BOUNTIFUL HARVEST

P9-DTA-533

PICTURED ON OUR COVER. Clockwise from top right: Stuffed Green Peppers (page 5), Garden Kabobs (page 18) and Fresh Strawberry Pie (page 79).

TOMATOES

*You can taste summer in every luscious bite of a red ripe tomato...
and these family-favorite recipes certainly prove it! Add some
color and tang to your table with these tantalizing tomato dishes.*

STUFFED GREEN PEPPERS

Helen Engelhart, Maplewood, Minnesota

(PICTURED AT LEFT AND ON COVER)

My family especially enjoys this dish in the summer when fresh tomatoes and green peppers are readily available. This recipe was given to me by my mother-in-law, and now when I visit my daughter and son-in-law, they always ask me to make it for them!

6 medium fresh tomatoes, peeled, seeded and
   chopped
1 medium onion, chopped
3 celery ribs, diced
1 can (8 ounces) tomato sauce
1 cup water
2 teaspoons salt, *divided*
1/2 teaspoon pepper, *divided*
4 medium green peppers
1 pound lean ground beef
1 cup instant rice, cooked
1 teaspoon dried basil

In a large saucepan or Dutch oven, combine tomatoes, onion, celery, tomato sauce, water, 1 teaspoon salt and 1/4 teaspoon pepper. Bring to a boil. Reduce heat and simmer 10-15 minutes. Meanwhile, cut tops off of green peppers and remove seeds; set aside. In a bowl, combine ground beef, rice, basil and remaining salt and pepper; mix well. Fill peppers with beef mixture. Carefully place peppers in tomato sauce. Spoon some sauce over tops of peppers. Cover and simmer for 40-45 minutes or until beef is cooked and peppers are tender. **Yield:** 4 servings.

FESTIVE TOMATO WEDGES

Wilma Purcell, Alma, Illinois

(PICTURED AT LEFT)

Since I have a large vegetable and herb garden, many of the ingredients in this recipe are truly "homegrown". I found this simple recipe in a magazine years ago and it quickly became a favorite at family picnics. I have five married children and seven grandchildren, and they all love to come home for some of "Mom's cooking".

6 medium fresh tomatoes, cored and cut into
   wedges
DRESSING:
2/3 cup vegetable oil
1/4 cup white wine vinegar
1/4 cup snipped fresh parsley
1/4 cup sliced green onions
1 garlic clove, minced
2 tablespoons mayonnaise
1 teaspoon dill weed
1 teaspoon dried basil
1 teaspoon salt
1/4 teaspoon pepper
1/4 teaspoon dried oregano

Place tomato wedges in a large bowl. Place all of the dressing ingredients in a blender or food processor; process until blended. Pour dressing over tomatoes and toss gently. Chill before serving. **Yield:** 12 servings.

SUMMER SPAGHETTI SALAD

August Salemi, Atascadero, California

(PICTURED AT LEFT)

Although tomatoes do not usually come to mind when someone mentions California, they are indeed one of our most plentiful crops. This chilled salad is particularly satisfying on hot summer days.

2 to 3 cups chopped fresh tomatoes
1/2 cup chopped fresh basil
1/4 cup chopped fresh oregano
1/4 cup chopped fresh parsley
1/2 cup chopped green onions
2 garlic cloves, minced
1 teaspoon salt
Pinch pepper
1/4 cup plus 1 tablespoon olive oil, *divided*
2 tablespoons red wine vinegar
Vermicilli *or* angel hair pasta
2 tablespoons grated Parmesan cheese

In a bowl, combine tomatoes with herbs, onions and garlic. Add salt, pepper, 1/4 cup olive oil and vinegar. Mix well; cover and chill. Cook pasta; drain. Toss in a bowl with Parmesan cheese and remaining olive oil. Cover and chill. Top each serving of pasta with sauce. **Yield:** 4-6 servings.

TERRIFIC TOMATOES. *Pictured at left, from the top: Stuffed Green Peppers, Festive Tomato Wedges and Summer Spaghetti Salad (all recipes on this page).*

RED RICE

Mildred Sherrer, Bay City, Texas

This colorful rice dish really bursts with the taste of bacon. Plus, the hot pepper sauce really adds spice!

- **5 bacon strips**
- **1 medium onion, diced**
- **2 cups chopped seeded peeled fresh tomatoes**
- **1 cup uncooked long grain rice**
- **1 cup tomato juice *or* water**
- **1 cup finely chopped fully cooked ham**
- **1/2 teaspoon salt**
- **1/8 teaspoon pepper**
- **1/8 teaspoon hot pepper sauce**

In a skillet, cook bacon until crisp. Remove bacon to paper towels to drain; discard all but 2 tablespoons of drippings. Saute onion in drippings until tender. Add bacon and remaining ingredients. Cook, covered, over medium-low heat for 10 minutes. Spoon into a 1-1/2-qt. baking dish. Cover and bake at 350° for 45 minutes or until rice is tender, stirring occasionally. **Yield:** 6 servings.

MILD FRESH SALSA

Rebecca Arce Bell, Holtville, California

This quick-and-easy salsa tastes great as an accompaniment to meat dishes as well as with chips. I teach kindergarten and my husband is a county Extension agent. We've lived down here in the Imperial Valley for 30 years. I say "down here" because Holtville is 15 feet below sea level!

- **3 fresh tomatoes, peeled, seeded and finely chopped**
- **1/2 cup finely chopped fresh cilantro *or* parsley**
- **2 to 3 garlic cloves, minced**
- **1 can (4 ounces) chopped green chilies**
- **1/2 cup sliced green onions**
- **1/2 teaspoon salt**
- **1/4 teaspoon pepper**

In a a bowl, combine all ingredients. Chill before serving. **Yield:** 3 cups.

GOULASH SOUP

Lois Teske, Buckley, Illinois

I found this recipe in a church cookbook and modified it slightly so it tastes just like the goulash soup we had while visiting Germany a few years ago. It's now become a family favorite at our house.

- **1-1/2 pounds lean beef stew meat, cut into 1-inch cubes**
- **2 pounds beef soup bones**
- **1 quart fresh tomatoes, peeled and chopped**
- **1 medium onion, chopped**
- **4 large potatoes, peeled and diced**
- **6 carrots, sliced**
- **3 celery ribs, sliced**

- **3 cups chopped cabbage**
- **3 tablespoons Worcestershire sauce**
- **2 to 4 teaspoons salt**
- **1/2 teaspoon pepper**
- **3 tablespoons minced fresh parsley**

In a large kettle or Dutch oven, cover stew meat and soup bones with water. Simmer, covered, about 2 hours or until meat is tender. Remove meat from bones; strain broth and discard bones. Return broth and meat to kettle. Add the next nine ingredients. Simmer, covered, about 1 hour or until vegetables are tender. Sprinkle with parsley. **Yield:** about 16 servings (4 quarts).

LENTIL SOUP

Joyce Pyra, North Battleford, Saskatchewan

This hearty soup can be easily doubled for big crowds. My family likes it topped with shredded cheddar cheese.

- **1 cup dry lentils, rinsed**
- **6 cups chicken broth**
- **2 cups chopped onion**
- **1 garlic clove, minced**
- **1 tablespoon cooking oil**
- **2-1/2 cups chopped fresh tomatoes**
- **1 cup sliced carrots**
- **1/2 teaspoon dried thyme**
- **1/4 teaspoon dried marjoram**

In a large saucepan, bring lentils and chicken broth to a boil. Reduce heat; simmer for 30 minutes. Meanwhile, in a skillet, saute onion and garlic in oil; add to saucepan. Add tomatoes, carrots, thyme and marjoram. Cook 30 minutes longer or until lentils and vegetables are tender. **Yield:** about 8 servings (2 quarts).

TOMATO VEGETABLE SOUP

Brenda Korinek, Manitowoc, Wisconsin

Gardening is one of my many hobbies and this recipe is a great way to use fresh tomatoes. It makes a wonderful light meal, served with crackers or herb-flavored croutons.

- **1 medium onion, chopped**
- **2 tablespoons butter *or* margarine**
- **4 cups water**
- **2-1/2 pounds fresh tomatoes, peeled and chopped**
- **2 medium carrots, diced**
- **1 celery rib, finely chopped**
- **3 chicken bouillon cubes**
- **1 teaspoon sugar**
- **1 teaspoon dried basil**
- **1/2 teaspoon salt**
- **1/2 teaspoon dried thyme**
- **1/8 teaspoon ground mace**
- **1/8 teaspoon pepper**

In a large saucepan, saute onion in butter until tender. Add remaining ingredients; bring to a boil. Reduce heat and simmer, covered, for 40 minutes or until vegetables are tender. **Yield:** about 8 servings (2 quarts).

TOMATO PASTA SALAD
Dorothy Evans, Cairo, Missouri

Because we grew so many nice big tomatoes last year, I created this recipe. The combination of the two different dressings really makes this pasta salad unique.

> 8 medium fresh tomatoes, diced
> 3 medium cucumbers, diced
> 2 medium green peppers, diced
> 1 medium onion, diced
> 1 cup chopped fully cooked ham
> 1 cup vegetable corkscrew noodles, cooked and drained
> 1 can (2-1/4 ounces) sliced ripe olives, drained
> 1/2 cup shredded cheddar cheese
> 1/2 cup ranch-style dressing
> 1/2 cup French dressing

Toss the first eight ingredients in a large bowl. Combine the dressings and stir into vegetable mixture. Chill before serving. **Yield:** 12-16 servings.

TOMATO-GARLIC DRESSING
Diane Hyatt, Renton, Washington

I've served this salad dressing many times when having company over for dinner and everyone just loves it. I've had this recipe for so many years, I forgot where it came from!

> 2 cups mayonnaise
> 1 teaspoon lemon juice
> 1 teaspoon garlic powder
> 2 medium tomatoes, cubed

Combine all ingredients in a food processor or blender. Process until smooth. Chill. **Yield:** about 3 cups.

DUMPLINGS WITH TOMATOES AND ZUCCHINI
Mildred Renfro, Lewiston, Michigan

Here's a unique and tasty side dish that has dumplings made with absolutely no flour!

> 1/4 cup chopped onion
> 2 tablespoons cooking oil
> 4 large fresh tomatoes, peeled and chopped
> 1 tablespoon minced fresh basil *or* 1 teaspoon dried basil
> 1 teaspoon sugar
> 1 teaspoon salt
> 1/4 teaspoon pepper
> 2 medium zucchini, peeled and cubed

PARMESAN DUMPLINGS:
> 1 egg, lightly beaten
> 1 cup grated Parmesan cheese

In a large skillet, saute onion in oil until tender. Add tomatoes, basil, sugar, salt and pepper. Simmer, covered, for 20 minutes. Add zucchini; cook, covered, for 15 minutes or until tender. For dumplings, combine egg and cheese. Drop by tablespoons onto tomato mixture. Simmer, covered, for 5 minutes or until dumplings are firm. *Editor's Note:* These dumplings *do not* contain flour. **Yield:** 6 servings.

FRIED GREEN TOMATOES
Judy Benson, Granite Falls, Minnesota

When I was growing up, these were a summertime favorite with my family. Back then, we just dipped the tomato slices in flour and fried them in butter.

> 1/2 cup all-purpose flour
> 1/4 cup cornmeal
> 1/4 cup grated Parmesan cheese
> 1/2 teaspoon dried oregano
> 1/2 teaspoon salt
> 1/8 teaspoon pepper
> 3 to 4 green tomatoes, cut into 1/2-inch slices

Cooking oil

Combine flour, cornmeal, Parmesan cheese, oregano, salt and pepper. Coat tomato slices with flour mixture. In a skillet, heat oil over medium. Fry tomatoes for 2-3 minutes per side until tender and lightly browned. Drain on paper towels. Serve immediately. **Yield:** 4-6 servings

TOMATO MUSHROOM SOUP
Bonnie Hawkins, Woodstock, Illinois

This soup recipe came about while I was experimenting with the goodies from my garden...I serve it often to my family, especially in the winter. We live in the country and raise horses, and I just love looking out my kitchen window at these fine animals as I cook!

> 1 pound fresh mushrooms, thinly sliced
> 6 tablespoons butter *or* margarine, *divided*
> 2 medium onions, minced
> 1 garlic clove, minced
> 2 carrots, chopped
> 3 celery ribs, finely chopped
> 3 tablespoons all-purpose flour
> 8 cups beef broth
> 2 tomatoes, peeled, seeded and chopped
> 1 can (15 ounces) tomato sauce
> 1 teaspoon salt
> 1/2 teaspoon pepper
> 3 tablespoons minced fresh parsley

Sour cream, optional

In a large kettle or Dutch oven, saute mushrooms in 4 tablespoons butter until tender. Remove mushrooms; set aside. In the same kettle, saute onions, garlic, carrots and celery in remaining butter until tender. Stir in flour until smooth. Add broth, tomatoes, tomato sauce, salt, pepper and half of the mushrooms. Simmer, covered, about 30 minutes. Add parsley and remaining mushrooms; simmer 5 minutes longer or until heated through. Garnish each serving with a dollop of sour cream if desired. **Yield:** about 12 servings (3 quarts).

RIPE WITH FLAVOR. *Clockwise from upper left: Zesty Tomato Zucchini Toss, Italian Garden Sauce, Stuffed Garden Tomatoes, Tomato Pepper Steak, Creamy Tomato Bisque and Tomato Dill Bread (all recipes on pages 10 and 11).*

STUFFED
GARDEN TOMATOES
Jessica Gambino, Waveland, Mississippi

(PICTURED ON PAGE 9)

These stuffed tomatoes make delicious use of vegetables straight from the garden. As a side dish, they're a mouth-watering complement to any meal.

- 4 medium fresh tomatoes
- 6 tablespoons butter *or* margarine, *divided*
- 1 medium carrot, coarsely chopped
- 8 radishes, coarsely chopped
- 2 green onions with tops, thinly sliced
- 1 small cucumber, peeled, seeded and coarsely chopped
- 1/2 cup fresh *or* frozen peas
- 1 tablespoon chopped fresh parsley
- 1/2 teaspoon dried oregano
- 2 garlic cloves, minced
- 1/2 teaspoon salt
- 4 teaspoons grated Parmesan cheese
- 4 teaspoons seasoned dry bread crumbs
- 1 teaspoon sugar

Cut a thin slice from top of each tomato. Leaving a 1/2-in.-thick shell, scoop out pulp and discard. Invert tomatoes onto paper towels to drain. Meanwhile, in a skillet, melt 4 tablespoons of the butter over medium-high heat. Saute carrot, radishes, green onions, cucumber, peas, parsley, oregano, garlic and salt until the vegetables are tender. Stuff tomatoes and place in a greased shallow baking dish. Melt remaining butter; stir in Parmesan cheese, bread crumbs and sugar. Sprinkle over tomatoes. Bake, uncovered, at 400° for 20 minutes or until crumbs are lightly browned. **Yield:** 4 servings.

TOMATO PEPPER STEAK
Carolyn Butterfield, Atkinson, Nebraska

(PICTURED ON PAGE 9)

We live on the eastern edge of the Sand Hills here in Nebraska, where most folks are ranchers. This popular beef dish is tasty as well as colorful.

- 1 pound round steak, cut into 1/4-inch x 2-inch strips
- 1 tablespoon paprika
- 2 tablespoons butter *or* margarine
- 1 can (10-1/2 ounces) beef broth
- 2 garlic cloves, minced
- 2 medium green peppers, cut into strips
- 1 cup thinly sliced onion
- 2 tablespoons cornstarch
- 2 tablespoons soy sauce
- 1/3 cup cold water
- 2 fresh tomatoes, peeled and cut into wedges
- Cooked rice

Sprinkle meat with paprika. In a large skillet, melt butter over medium-high heat. Brown beef. Add broth and garlic.

Simmer, covered, for 30 minutes. Add green peppers and onion. Cover and continue to simmer for 5 minutes. Combine cornstarch, soy sauce and water; stir into meat mixture. Cook and stir until thickened. Gently stir in tomatoes and heat through. Serve over rice. **Yield:** 4-6 servings.

ZESTY TOMATO
ZUCCHINI TOSS
Ann Shorey, Sutherlin, Oregon

(PICTURED ON PAGE 8)

Summer barbecues at our 10-acre spread usually include this tangy salad because it goes so well with grilled meat. Everyone loves the flavor—I know this for a fact because they always come back for seconds!

- 6 medium fresh tomatoes, sliced
- 3 medium zucchini, sliced
- 1 medium red onion, sliced into rings
- 1/4 cup minced fresh parsley

DRESSING:
- 2/3 cup vegetable oil
- 1/2 cup white wine vinegar
- 2 teaspoons minced fresh basil
- 1 teaspoon salt
- 1/2 teaspoon pepper
- 1/4 teaspoon garlic powder

In a large bowl, layer tomatoes, zucchini, onion and parsley. Whisk together dressing ingredients; pour over vegetables. Chill before serving. **Yield:** 10-12 servings.

FOR BEST FLAVOR, *purchase tomatoes ripened on the vine in an area near you. Those shipped long distances are picked green and are less flavorful as they ripen in stores.*

TOMATO DILL BREAD
Chris Bowman, Enterprise, Oregon

(PICTURED ON PAGE 8)

Delicately flavored with various herbs, this bread disappears fast at our home here in the beautiful Wallowa Mountains of Oregon. It also makes great sandwiches.

- 1 package (1/4 ounce) active dry yeast
- 2 tablespoons sugar
- 1/2 cup warm water (110° to 115°)
- 1-1/2 cups chopped peeled tomatoes
- 2 tablespoons vegetable oil
- 1 tablespoon minced fresh parsley
- 1 tablespoon minced fresh dill
- 1 tablespoon minced fresh oregano
- 2 teaspoons salt
- 3-1/2 to 4-1/2 cups all-purpose flour
- 3 tablespoons butter *or* margarine, melted

In a large bowl, dissolve yeast and sugar in water; set aside.

In a blender or food processor, puree tomatoes with oil, parsley, dill, oregano and salt. Add to yeast mixture. Add enough flour to make a smooth dough. Turn onto a floured surface; knead until smooth and elastic, about 6-8 minutes. Place in a greased bowl, turning once to grease top. Cover and let rise in a warm place until doubled, about 1 hour. Punch down and divide in half; shape into loaves. Place into two greased 8-in. x 4-in. x 2-in. loaf pans. Cover and let rise until doubled, about 1 hour. Bake at 400° for 15 minutes. Reduce heat to 350°; bake for 25 minutes longer or until done. Brush with melted butter. **Yield:** 2 loaves.

ITALIAN GARDEN SAUCE
Deborah Hill, Coffeyville, Kansas
(PICTURED ON PAGE 9)

Although we plant a medium-size garden each year, we grow lots of tomatoes. This sauce is especially good because it's so chunky...and goes well with all kinds of pasta.

- **1 pound bulk Italian sausage**
- **8 cups diced peeled fresh tomatoes**
- **2 medium green peppers, diced**
- **1 large onion, diced**
- **1 to 2 garlic cloves, minced**
- **1 can (15 ounces) tomato sauce**
- **1-1/2 cups water**
- **2 tablespoons dried parsley flakes**
- **1 tablespoon dried oregano**
- **1 tablespoon dried basil**
- **1 tablespoon Italian seasoning**
- **1 teaspoon salt**
- **Cooked pasta**

In a large Dutch oven, brown and crumble sausage; drain. Add tomatoes, green peppers, onion, garlic, tomato sauce, water and seasonings. Cook, uncovered, for 2-1/2 hours or until sauce reaches desired thickness. Serve over pasta. **Yield:** about 9 cups.

CREAMY TOMATO BISQUE
Cathy Fulton, Hazlet, New Jersey
(PICTURED ON PAGE 8)

This rich, creamy bisque has a wonderful old-fashioned flavor...it makes a nice accompaniment to any meal.

- **2 cups water**
- **4 chicken bouillon cubes**
- **1 can (15-1/2 ounces) tomatoes with liquid, cut up**
- **1/2 cup chopped celery**
- **2 tablespoons chopped onion**
- **2 medium fresh tomatoes, peeled and diced**
- **1/4 cup butter *or* margarine**
- **3 tablespoons all-purpose flour**
- **2 cups light cream**
- **1/3 to 1/2 cup sherry, optional**

In a large saucepan, bring first five ingredients to a boil. Reduce heat; cover and simmer for 15-20 minutes or until vegetables are tender. Cool. Puree mixture in a food pro-

cessor or blender; set aside. In the same saucepan, saute fresh tomatoes in butter for 5 minutes. Stir in flour to make a smooth paste. Gradually add cream and stir over low heat until thickened. Stir in pureed mixture and sherry if desired. **Yield:** about 8 servings (2 quarts).

GREEN TOMATO MINCEMEAT
Judy Outlaw, Huntsville, Alabama

We've just recently moved to Alabama from Portland, Oregon where we had an abundance of homegrown green tomatoes. This recipe came from a dear friend who has since passed on...I know she would be pleased that I'm sharing it here.

- **2 quarts (about 5 pounds) finely chopped green tomatoes**
- **1 quart finely chopped peeled tart apples (4 to 5)**
- **1-1/4 cups golden raisins**
- **1-1/4 cups packed brown sugar**
- **1-1/4 cups sugar**
- **1 cup water**
- **1/3 cup vinegar**
- **1/8 to 1/4 cup lemon juice**
- **2 tablespoons minced orange *or* lemon peel**
- **1-1/2 teaspoons ground cinnamon**
- **1 teaspoon salt**
- **1/8 teaspoon ground allspice**
- **1/8 teaspoon ground cloves**

Place all ingredients in a large kettle or Dutch oven. Bring to a boil. Reduce heat and simmer until thickened or mincemeat reaches desired consistency. Pack hot into hot jars, leaving 1/2-in. headspace. Adjust caps. Process for 25 minutes in a boiling-water bath. **Yield:** about 6 pints.

PICKLED TOMATO SALAD
Gene Swiderski, Bloomington, Minnesota

I've been cooking for my family for 40 years and love to experiment with different recipes. You may want to add a can of kidney beans for variation.

- **3 large tomatoes, cut into eighths**
- **1 medium green pepper, chopped**
- **1 medium red onion, thinly sliced into rings**
- **2 tablespoons minced fresh basil**
- **1/2 cup frozen apple juice concentrate, thawed**
- **1/2 cup cider vinegar**
- **1/4 teaspoon salt**
- **1 tablespoon vegetable oil**
- **1 teaspoon sugar**
- **1 tablespoon pickling spices, tied in a cheesecloth bag**

In a bowl, combine tomatoes, green pepper, onion and basil; set aside. In a saucepan, bring remaining ingredients to a boil. Reduce heat and simmer for 5 minutes. Remove pickling spices; cool to room temperature. Pour over vegetables. Cover and refrigerate at least 1 hour before serving. **Yield:** 6 servings.

VEGETABLE APPETIZER PIZZA
Marcia Tiernan, Madrid, New York
(PICTURED AT RIGHT)

My sister brought this recipe with her when she was visiting from California. We served it at a family get-together and everyone just loved it. We're often asked to bring it to potlucks.

 3 tubes (8 ounces *each*) refrigerated crescent rolls
 2 packages (8 ounces *each*) cream cheese, softened
2/3 cup mayonnaise
 1 tablespoon dill weed
 4 fresh tomatoes, seeded and chopped
 2 cups chopped fresh broccoli
 3 green onions, thinly sliced
 2 cups sliced fresh mushrooms
1/2 medium green pepper, chopped
1/2 medium sweet red pepper, chopped
 1 can (2-1/4 ounces) sliced ripe olives, drained
 2 cups (8 ounces) shredded cheddar cheese

Unroll crescent roll dough and place on two greased 15-in. x 10-in. x 1-in. baking pans. Flatten dough, sealing seams and perforations. Bake at 400° for 10 minutes or until light golden brown. Cool. In a small bowl, blend cream cheese, mayonnaise and dill. Spread over crusts. Top with vegetables, olives and cheese. Cut into bite-size squares. Refrigerate until ready to serve. **Yield:** about 96 appetizer servings.

TOMATO-PEPPER SALSA
Joanna Krentz, Lumsden, Saskatchewan
(PICTURED AT RIGHT)

My husband and I live on 160 acres of rich fertile soil, and every year I find myself inventing new recipes to use up the all the tomatoes we grow. This delicious salsa is one of them.

 4 cups chopped peeled fresh tomatoes
 2 cups chopped green pepper
 2 cups chopped sweet red pepper
 1 cup chopped onion
 1 to 2 cups seeded chopped jalapeno peppers
3/4 cup cider vinegar
 2 garlic cloves, minced
 1 tablespoon sugar
 1 tablespoon salt
 1 teaspoon paprika
 1 teaspoon dried oregano
 1 can (6 ounces) tomato paste
1/4 cup chopped fresh cilantro *or* parsley

In a large saucepan, combine first 11 ingredients; bring to a boil. Reduce heat and simmer, uncovered, for 1 hour or until mixture thickens. Stir in tomato paste and cilantro or

parsley. Simmer 5-10 minutes longer. Pour hot into hot jars, leaving 1/4-in. headspace. Adjust caps. Process for 30 minutes in a boiling-water bath. **Yield:** 3 pints.

GAZPACHO
Robynn Shannon, Alexandria, Virginia
(PICTURED AT RIGHT)

Nothing equals the taste of an ice-cold bowl of gazpacho on a hot summer day—I was hooked from the first spoonful! I found this recipe when I was looking for something to make with the abundance of tomatoes from my garden.

 1 medium green pepper, finely chopped
 2 celery ribs, finely chopped
 1 medium cucumber, peeled, seeded and finely chopped
1/4 cup minced fresh parsley
 1 tablespoon minced fresh chives
 1 garlic clove, minced
 1 green onion, thinly sliced
1/3 cup red wine vinegar
1/4 cup olive oil
 1 teaspoon salt
1/2 teaspoon pepper
1/2 teaspoon Worcestershire sauce
 3 cups chopped seeded peeled fresh tomatoes
 1 can (46 ounces) tomato juice
Seasoned croutons

In a large bowl, combine all ingredients except croutons. Chill for several hours or overnight. Garnish each serving with croutons. **Yield:** about 10 servings (2-1/2 quarts).

QUICK ZESTY CHILI
Laura Whitcomb, Wauseon, Ohio

This chili always has everyone coming back for seconds—that's because I use fresh tomatoes in the recipe. I've been married 31 years and our two grown children still like to come home to eat "Mom's cooking"!

 1 pound ground beef
 2 cans (15-1/2 ounces *each*) kidney beans, rinsed and drained
 1 can (8 ounces) tomato sauce
 2 cups chopped fresh tomatoes
 1 cup water
 2 tablespoons chili powder
 1 tablespoon dried minced onion
 1 to 2 teaspoons hot pepper sauce
 1 teaspoon ground cumin
1/4 teaspoon ground cinnamon

In a large saucepan, brown beef; drain. Add remaining ingredients. Bring to a boil; reduce heat and simmer for 15 minutes. **Yield:** 8 servings (2 quarts).

TOMATO TIME. *Pictured at right, clockwise from lower left: Gazpacho, Vegetable Appetizer Pizza and Tomato-Pepper Salsa (all recipes on this page).*

HERBED TOMATO AND CHEESE SALAD

Sharon Miller, Olivenhain, California

A flavorful combination of ingredients and a tangy garlic-laced dressing makes this salad a mouth-watering delight.

     5 large fresh tomatoes, cut into wedges
     1 medium green pepper, chopped
     1/2 small red onion, thinly sliced
  1-1/2 cups (6 ounces) shredded Monterey Jack cheese
     1/4 cup stuffed green olives, sliced
     1/2 teaspoon dried basil
DRESSING:
     6 tablespoons vegetable oil
     2 tablespoons red wine vinegar
     2 tablespoons minced fresh parsley
     1 tablespoon minced fresh chives
     1 garlic clove, minced
     1/2 teaspoon salt
     1/4 teaspoon pepper

Place tomato wedges in a shallow dish. Cover with green pepper, onion, cheese and olives. Sprinkle with basil. In a small bowl, mix dressing ingredients. Spoon over salad. **Yield:** 6-8 servings.

GARLIC-KISSED TOMATOES

Margaret Zickert, Deerfield, Wisconsin

Everyone I know loves this recipe—even my husband who normally doesn't like garlic! These tomatoes are a hit at potlucks...folks always ask for the recipe.

     6 medium fresh tomatoes
     1/4 cup vegetable oil
     2 garlic cloves, thinly sliced
     3 tablespoons lemon juice
     1/2 teaspoon dried oregano
     1/2 teaspoon salt
     1/8 teaspoon pepper

Peel and cut tomatoes in half horizontally. Squeeze tomatoes lightly to release seeds. Discard seeds and juices. Place tomato halves in a container with a tight-fitting lid. In a small bowl, mix the oil, garlic, lemon juice, oregano, salt and pepper. Pour over tomatoes. Seal lid and invert to thoroughly coat. Refrigerate at least 4 hours or up to 2 days, inverting occasionally to marinate. **Yield:** 12 servings.

TOMATO GARDEN CASSEROLE

Vera Laing, Marshall, Michigan

Here's an attractive tomato casserole that's both quick and easy to prepare...and tastes great, too!

     3 cups fresh tomato wedges
     1 cup (4 ounces) shredded cheddar cheese
     1 cup dry bread crumbs
     1 cup chopped green pepper
     1 small onion, diced
     1/4 cup butter *or* margarine, melted
     1/2 teaspoon salt
Dash paprika

In a large bowl, combine all of the ingredients. Spoon into a greased 1-1/2-qt. baking dish. Bake at 300° for 45 minutes or until vegetables are tender. **Yield:** 4 servings.

GREEN TOMATO CHOWCHOW

Selma Sherrill, Charlotte, North Carolina

Find yourself with a bumper crop of green tomatoes? Here's a terrific recipe that uses a full gallon of those green goodies from your garden. Try adding jalapeno peppers for a spicy "kick" to this crunchy relish.

     1 gallon green tomatoes (about 5 pounds)
     3 medium sweet red peppers
     3 medium green peppers
     4 large onions
     1 large head cabbage
     3 to 4 jalapeno peppers, optional
     3 cups sugar
     3 cups vinegar
     1/4 cup salt
  1-1/2 teaspoons celery seed
     1/2 teaspoon whole allspice
     1/2 teaspoon pepper
     1/2 teaspoon ground turmeric
     1/2 teaspoon chili powder

Coarsely chop tomatoes, red and green peppers, onions, cabbage and jalapeno peppers if desired. Place in a large kettle or Dutch oven; stir. Add remaining ingredients. Bring to a boil; reduce heat and simmer 30 minutes, stirring occasionally. Pack hot into hot jars, leaving 1/2-in. headspace. Adjust caps. Process for 10 minutes in a boiling-water bath. **Yield:** about 12 pints.

TUNA-STUFFED TOMATOES

Ellen Lloyd, Greenfield, Wisconsin

Here's a real treat for tuna (and tomato) lovers! Try topping these broiled tomatoes with cheddar cheese for a different taste.

     2 cans (6-1/8 ounces *each*) water-packed tuna, drained
     1/2 cup seasoned dry bread crumbs
     1/4 cup chopped onion
     1/4 teaspoon dry mustard
     1/4 teaspoon cayenne pepper
     1/2 teaspoon Italian seasoning
     1 egg, beaten
     4 medium fresh tomatoes
     1 cup (4 ounces) shredded mozzarella cheese
Sour cream, optional

In a bowl, separate tuna into very small pieces. Add bread crumbs, onion, mustard, cayenne pepper, Italian seasoning and egg; mix well. In a medium saucepan, cook mixture for 2-3 minutes over medium heat. Set aside. Slice off 1/2 in. of each tomato top. Leaving a 1/4-in.-thick shell, scoop out pulp and discard. Spoon tuna mixture into shells and place in a baking dish. Top with mozzarella cheese and brown lightly under broiler. Garnish with sour cream if desired. **Yield:** 4 servings.

TOMATO BEEF AND RICE CASSEROLE
Linda Bangert, Edwardsville, Illinois

Here's a delicious dish that is very easy to make—and fast, too. The best thing, though, is that you mix everything in one bowl!

> 1 pound lean ground beef
> 3 cups chopped canned tomatoes with liquid
> 1 medium green pepper, chopped
> 1 cup uncooked long grain rice
> 1 large onion, chopped
> 1 teaspoon chili powder
> 1/2 teaspoon salt
> 1/4 teaspoon pepper

In a large bowl, combine all ingredients. Place in a greased 2-qt. casserole. Bake, covered, at 400° for 1-1/2 hours, stirring once or twice. Remove cover during the last 15 minutes to brown. **Yield:** 6 servings.

WHEN CANNING *fresh tomatoes, always add 2 tablespoons bottled lemon juice to each quart before packing and processing in a boiling-water bath.*

BEEF TOMATO STIR-FRY
Shari Running, Seattle, Washington

I make this recipe often, especially in the summer when we harvest our garden and have an "oversupply" of tomatoes. This stir-fry always receives rave reviews from dinner guests.

> 1/2 pound flank steak *or* round steak
> 1-1/2 teaspoons minced fresh gingerroot
> 1 garlic clove, minced
> 4 teaspoons cornstarch, *divided*
> 1 teaspoon soy sauce
> 1 egg white
> 1 tablespoon vegetable oil
> 1 medium green pepper, cut into strips
> 1 medium onion, cut into strips
> 1 celery rib, sliced
> 1/2 cup plus 2 tablespoons water, *divided*

> 1/4 cup ketchup
> 3 tablespoons sugar
> 4 medium fresh tomatoes, peeled, seeded and cut into wedges
> 3 cups cooked rice

Slice steak on the diagonal into very thin strips. (It slices more easily if partially frozen.) In a bowl, mix gingerroot, garlic, 1 teaspoon cornstarch, soy sauce and egg white. Add the meat and toss to coat. Set aside for 5 minutes. In a large skillet or wok, heat oil on high; stir-fry the meat just until redness is gone. Remove the meat; set aside. Add the green pepper, onion, celery and 1/2 cup water; cover and cook over medium heat for 3 minutes. Add ketchup and sugar; cover and cook for 2 minutes. In a small bowl, mix remaining cornstarch and water. Stir into beef mixture; return to skillet. Cook until liquid is slightly thickened. Add tomatoes and stir for 1 minute just until heated through. Serve over rice. **Yield:** 4 servings.

TOMATO LEEK SOUP
Lois McAtee, Oceanside, California

This recipe was given to me years ago from a friend in Australia. We're a family that loves soup, and this recipe is one of our favorites.

> 3 leeks, finely sliced
> 5 cups chicken broth
> 2 pounds fresh tomatoes, peeled and chopped
> 1 teaspoon minced fresh basil *or* 1/4 teaspoon dried basil
> 1/2 teaspoon lemon pepper
> 1/4 teaspoon salt

In a saucepan, bring leeks and broth to a boil. Boil for 5 minutes. Add tomatoes. Reduce heat; simmer for 10 minutes. Stir in basil, lemon pepper and salt. **Yield:** 6-8 servings (2 quarts).

TOMATO/ZUCCHINI PASTA SUPPER
Donna Kohls, New Berlin, Wisconsin

The hearty, full taste of fresh ingredients makes this dish as delicious as any you'll find in a fancy restaurant. My family loves it!

> 1 medium onion, chopped
> 2 garlic cloves, minced
> 1/4 cup olive oil
> 2 cups cubed peeled fresh tomatoes
> 4 small zucchini, julienned
> 2 tablespoons chopped fresh basil
> 1/2 teaspoon salt
> 1/4 teaspoon pepper
> 1 pound linguini *or* spaghetti, cooked and drained

In a large skillet, saute onion and garlic in oil until tender. Add tomatoes and zucchini; saute until tender. Add basil, salt and pepper. Serve over hot pasta. **Yield:** 2-4 servings.

SQUASH

*These recipes provide some surefire ways to make
the most of your squash harvest—from Acorn to Zucchini!*

ZUCCHINI PROVENCAL

Bobbie Jo Yokley, Franklin, Kentucky

(PICTURED AT LEFT)

My sister created this recipe and shared it with me. She has a huge vegetable garden and each year works with her abundant yield, combining her vegetables in many different ways. Somehow, she always seems to come up with a new dish that's both colorful and delicious!

    1 small onion, chopped
    2 tablespoons cooking oil
    2 medium zucchini, cubed
    1/3 cup diced green pepper
    1 garlic clove, minced
    1/4 teaspoon salt
    1/8 teaspoon pepper
    2 large tomatoes, peeled and quartered
    1/4 cup grated Parmesan cheese
    1 tablespoon snipped fresh parsley

In a skillet, saute onion in oil until tender. Stir in zucchini, green pepper, garlic, salt and pepper. Cover and cook over low heat 5-6 minutes or until vegetables are almost tender. Stir in tomatoes; heat through. Transfer to a serving platter and sprinkle with Parmesan cheese and parsley. Serve immediately. **Yield:** 4-6 servings.

ITALIAN ZUCCHINI SOUP

Clara Mae Chambers, Superior, Nebraska

(PICTURED AT LEFT)

This recipe was given to me by my neighbor. Nice and simple, it's a good way to use a lot of your zucchini and other garden vegetables. It freezes well and is great to have on hand on a cold winter day.

    1 pound bulk Italian sausage
    1 cup chopped onion
    2 cups chopped celery
    1 medium green pepper, chopped

ZUCCHINI WITH ZEST. *Pictured at left, clockwise from the top: Zucchini Provencal, Italian Zucchini Soup and Onion Zucchini Bread (all recipes on this page).*

    2 to 4 tablespoons sugar
    2 teaspoons salt
    1/2 teaspoon dried basil
    1/2 teaspoon dried oregano
    1/2 teaspoon pepper
    1 quart canned tomatoes, cut up
    4 cups diced zucchini
Grated Parmesan cheese, optional

In a Dutch oven, brown sausage with onion; drain excess fat. Add the next eight ingredients; cover and simmer 1 hour. Stir in zucchini and simmer 10 minutes. Sprinkle with Parmesan cheese if desired. **Yield:** 2 quarts.

ONION ZUCCHINI BREAD

Annie Sassard, Ft. McCoy, Florida

(PICTURED AT LEFT)

Only two steps and this bread is mixed and ready for the oven! We love the flavor of the onion and Parmesan cheese. Baked in a round pan, it looks nice on the table whole or sliced in wedges.

    3 cups all-purpose flour
    3/4 cup chopped onion
    1/2 cup grated Parmesan cheese, *divided*
    5 teaspoons baking powder
    1 teaspoon salt
    1/2 teaspoon baking soda
    1 cup buttermilk
    1/3 cup vegetable oil
    2 eggs, lightly beaten
    3/4 cup finely shredded zucchini

In a bowl, combine flour, onion, 6 tablespoons of Parmesan cheese, baking powder, salt and baking soda. In a small bowl, mix buttermilk, oil, eggs and zucchini; stir into flour mixture just until blended. Spoon into a greased 9-in. round baking pan. Sprinkle with remaining Parmesan. Bake at 350° for 40 minutes. **Yield:** 6-8 servings.

CURRIED ZUCCHINI SOUP

Ruth McCombie, Etobicoke, Ontario

This soup, a recipe given to me by one of my daughters-in-law, is a special treat when used from the freezer on a cold winter's day. It calls to mind memories of the "zucchini summer" that was—and gives hope of the "zucchini summer" yet to be!

 2 pounds zucchini, sliced (about 4 medium)
 5 green onions, chopped
 4 cups chicken broth
 1 to 2 tablespoons butter *or* margarine, optional
 1-1/2 teaspoons curry powder
 1 teaspoon salt
 1/8 teaspoon cayenne pepper

In a large saucepan or Dutch oven, combine all ingredients. Simmer, covered, until zucchini is soft, about 15 minutes. Puree in batches in a blender on low speed; return to pan and heat through. **Yield:** 6-8 servings (2 quarts).

ZUCCHINI BISQUE

Marjorie Beck, Sonora, California

I like to serve this soup as a first course for special dinners. It is nice and light, pretty in color and very appetizing with its blend of flavors.

 1 medium onion, diced
 1/2 cup butter *or* margarine
 2-1/2 cups shredded zucchini
 2-1/2 cups chicken broth
 1/2 teaspoon dried basil
 1/2 teaspoon salt
 1/2 teaspoon pepper
 1/4 teaspoon ground nutmeg
 1 cup light cream

In a large saucepan, saute onion in butter. Add zucchini and chicken broth. Simmer, covered, for about 15 minutes; add seasonings. Puree on low in a blender. Return to pan; stir in cream and heat through. **Yield:** 4-5 servings (5 cups).

ZUCCHINI CAKE

Carolyn Sellers, Seminole, Oklahoma

This recipe came from my mother, whom I still proclaim as one of the best cooks in the country! Every time I serve it, it brings back memories of all the good old-fashioned cakes she lovingly prepared.

 3 cups all-purpose flour
 3 cups sugar
 2-1/2 teaspoons ground cinnamon
 1-1/2 teaspoons baking soda
 1 teaspoon salt
 1-1/2 cups vegetable oil
 4 eggs, lightly beaten
 1 teaspoon vanilla extract

 3 cups shredded zucchini
 1 cup chopped walnuts
FROSTING:
 1 package (8 ounces) cream cheese, softened
 1/2 cup butter *or* margarine, softened
 4 cups (1 pound) confectioners' sugar
 1 teaspoon vanilla extract

In a mixing bowl, combine flour, sugar, cinnamon, baking soda and salt. In a separate bowl, mix oil, eggs and vanilla; add to flour mixture and beat. Add zucchini; mix well. Fold in nuts. Pour into three well-greased 9-in. baking pans. Bake at 325° for 30-40 minutes or until cakes test done. Let stand 10 minutes; remove from pans and cool on wire racks. For frosting, beat cream cheese and butter; blend in sugar and vanilla. Beat until smooth. Frost between layers and top and sides of cake. **Yield:** 10-12 servings.

GARDEN KABOBS

Lorri Cleveland, Kingsville, Ohio
(PICTURED ON COVER)

When my garden is at its peak, I like to make this colorful entree. Besides the great flavor, I also enjoy its easy preparation and cleanup.

 1/4 cup vegetable oil
 1/4 cup lemon juice
 1/4 cup soy sauce
 1/4 cup packed brown sugar
 2 garlic cloves, minced
 3 whole cloves
Dash dried basil
 2-1/2 pounds pork tenderloin *or* sirloin steak, cut into 1-1/4-inch pieces
 2 dozen cherry tomatoes
 2 dozen fresh mushroom caps
 1 large green *or* sweet red pepper, cut into 1-1/2-inch cubes
 2 small zucchini, cut into 1-inch slices
 1 medium onion, cut into wedges
Cooked rice

In a bowl, combine first seven ingredients; set aside. Assemble kabobs by threading meat and vegetables on metal skewers. Place in a large glass dish. Pour marinade over kabobs; cover and refrigerate 6 hours or overnight. Turn several times. To cook, grill kabobs over hot coals until the meat and vegetables have reached desired doneness. Remove from the skewers and serve over rice. **Yield:** 10 servings.

PICNIC ZUCCHINI BEAN SALAD

Jane Colle, Sterling, Kansas

This is one of my newest recipes (I trade salad recipes with my husband's aunt in Nebraska). I've found that it's a pretty salad and easy to pack up for picnics in hot weather.

 3 small zucchini, sliced
 3/4 cup chopped green pepper

1/2 cup chopped onion
1 can (15-1/2 ounces) kidney beans, rinsed and drained
1/4 cup vegetable oil
3 tablespoons vinegar
1-1/2 teaspoons garlic salt
1/4 teaspoon pepper

In a bowl, combine all ingredients. Cover and refrigerate at least 4 hours, stirring occasionally. **Yield:** 5 cups.

ACORN CABBAGE BAKE

Alene Lundberg, Cedar Falls, Iowa

I have served this variation of squash often. It's a nice side dish, especially appropriate in the fall—or it can be used for a main luncheon dish. If you prepare your squash ahead and freeze it, it takes very little time to put this recipe together.

2 large acorn squash
1 tablespoon butter *or* margarine
2 cups shredded cabbage
1 medium onion, chopped
1 medium apple, chopped
1/2 pound pork sausage, cooked and drained
2 tablespoons slivered almonds
3/4 teaspoon salt
1/2 teaspoon ground sage
1/4 teaspoon ground thyme
1/4 teaspoon pepper

Cut squash in half; remove seeds. Place with cut side down in a 13-in. x 9-in. x 2-in. baking dish. Add 1/2 in. of water to pan. Cover and bake at 400° for 20 minutes or until tender. Cool; scoop out pulp (should have about 4 cups). In a large skillet over medium heat, melt butter. Saute cabbage, onion and apple until tender, about 5 minutes. Add sausage, almonds, salt, sage, thyme and pepper; mix well. Remove from heat and add squash. Place in a greased 2-qt. casserole. Bake at 350° for 30 minutes or until heated through. **Yield:** 8 servings.

MICROWAVE SPAGHETTI SQUASH

Lina Vainauskas, Shaw Air Force Base, South Carolina

One of the pleasant surprises about squash is that it's so low in calories. That means I can "splurge" a little with the other ingredients. Spaghetti squash is fun to work with and so "tender tasty"!

1 spaghetti squash (about 1-1/2 pounds)
1 medium sweet red pepper, thinly sliced
1 small onion, thinly sliced
2 garlic cloves, minced
1 tablespoon olive oil
1 medium tomato, chopped
1 medium zucchini, thinly sliced
1 cup sliced mushrooms
1 tablespoon tarragon vinegar
1 teaspoon dried tarragon
1/2 teaspoon salt
1/4 teaspoon pepper

Pierce squash with a fork. Place on paper towel in microwave; cook on high for 6 minutes per pound or until squash is soft. Let stand 5-10 minutes. Cut in half; remove seeds and scoop out pulp. Set aside. In a 2-qt. casserole, toss red pepper, onion, garlic and olive oil. Cover and microwave on high for 2 minutes or until slightly soft. Add tomato, zucchini, mushrooms, vinegar, tarragon, salt and pepper. Cover and microwave on high for 3 minutes or until crisp-tender. Toss with squash and serve immediately. **Yield:** 6-8 servings.

ZUCCHINI PEACH JELLY

Ruth Glick, Apple Creek, Ohio

I like to use this jelly as a condiment. It's always a conversation piece...everyone wonders about the "green" ingredient! This beautiful jelly is so easy to make and I often use it as a gift-giving item for the holidays.

6 cups shredded peeled zucchini (about 4 medium)
6 cups sugar
2 tablespoons lemon juice
1 can (8 ounces) crushed pineapple with juice
2 packages (3 ounces *each*) peach-flavored gelatin

In a large saucepan or Dutch oven, combine zucchini, sugar, lemon juice and pineapple with juice; bring to a boil. Cook, stirring often, at a full boil for 10 minutes. Remove from the heat; stir in gelatin. Spoon into clean jelly jars. Cover and cool. Store in the refrigerator. **Yield:** 7-1/2 pints.

HOLIDAY SQUASH

Kay Cripe, Wiri, South Auckland, New Zealand

This recipe came from our youngest daughter who especially likes to prepare it at Christmas. The crunchy topping and touch of sweet maple syrup make it our favorite side dish for turkey or ham.

3/4 cup all-purpose flour
3/4 cup packed brown sugar
2 teaspoons ground cinnamon
1 teaspoon ground allspice
1/4 teaspoon salt
1/2 cup butter *or* margarine
1 butternut squash (about 3 pounds)
1 cup chopped pecans
1 cup maple syrup

In a medium bowl, combine flour, brown sugar, cinnamon, allspice and salt; cut in butter until crumbly. Peel squash; cut into 1/2-in. slices, removing seeds when necessary. Put a third of the squash slices in a greased 11-in. x 7-in. x 2-in. baking dish. Sprinkle with 3/4 cup crumb mixture. Layer the remaining squash on top, overlapping when necessary. Sprinkle remaining crumb mixture over top. Top with pecans. Drizzle with maple syrup. Cover with foil; bake at 350° for 1 hour. Remove foil; bake 10 minutes more or until squash is done. **Yield:** 10-12 servings.

VERSATILE VEGETABLE. *Clockwise from upper right: Sweet-and-Sour Zucchini, Zucchini Pizza, Squash and Potatoes, Butternut Squash Casserole and Zucchini Hamburger Pie (all recipes on pages 22 and 23).*

ZUCCHINI PIZZA

Joyce Sitz, Wichita, Kansas

(PICTURED ON PAGE 21)

Everyone enjoys the flavor of this delicious and different way to serve zucchini. It is a healthy, quick meal to prepare and a change from what we know as pizza. I serve it quite often to my guests and they can never guess what the "secret ingredient" is!

> 3 cups shredded zucchini
> 3 eggs, well beaten
> 1/3 cup all-purpose flour
> 1-1/2 teaspoons dried oregano, *divided*
> 1 teaspoon dried basil, *divided*
> 1/4 teaspoon salt
> 1 cup sliced ripe olives
> 2/3 cup sliced green onions with tops
> 1/2 cup chopped green pepper
> 2 cups (8 ounces) shredded mozzarella cheese
> 2 to 3 medium tomatoes, peeled and thinly sliced

Press excess liquid from zucchini and place in a bowl. Add eggs, flour, 1/2 teaspoon oregano, 1/2 teaspoon basil and salt; mix well. Spread evenly over the bottom of a greased 13-in. x 9-in. x 2-in. baking dish. Bake at 450° for 8-10 minutes. Remove from oven and cool on a wire rack. Reduce heat to 350°. Sprinkle zucchini crust with olives, green onions, green pepper, cheese, and remaining oregano and basil. Cover with tomato slices. Bake for 25-30 minutes or until cheese is bubbly. Cool on wire rack 5 minutes before cutting. **Yield:** 6-8 servings.

BUTTERNUT SQUASH NUT CAKE

Margaret Connor, Austin, Texas

This cake is my favorite to bake because it brings back warm memories of a dear friend who gave me the recipe. And since it's my husband's favorite to eat, I make it often. It's usually my first choice when I'm asked to bring a dish for potlucks, and it's always a hit.

> 3 cups all-purpose flour
> 2 teaspoons baking powder
> 3/4 teaspoon baking soda
> 1-1/2 teaspoons ground cinnamon
> 1/2 teaspoon salt
> 1/2 teaspoon ground nutmeg
> 1/4 teaspoon ground cloves
> 1 cup butter *or* margarine, softened
> 1-3/4 cups sugar
> 3 eggs
> 1-1/3 cups pureed winter squash
> 1/2 cup milk
> 3/4 cup chopped pecans

BROWN SUGAR FROSTING:
> 1 cup packed dark brown sugar
> 1/2 cup butter *or* margarine
> 1/3 cup heavy cream
> 1 teaspoon vanilla extract

> 1-1/4 cups confectioners' sugar

Combine first seven ingredients; set aside. In a large mixing bowl, cream butter and sugar. Add eggs, one at a time, beating well after each addition. Add squash; mix well. (Mixture will appear curdled.) Alternately add dry ingredients and milk. Stir in pecans. Pour batter into a greased and floured 10-in. tube pan. Bake at 350° for 1 hour or until cake tests done. Cool in pan about 45 minutes. Remove from pan and cool on wire rack. For frosting, combine brown sugar, butter and cream in a medium saucepan; bring to a boil. Cook and stir for 2 minutes. Remove from the heat; stir in vanilla. Transfer to a mixing bowl; cool to lukewarm. Gradually beat in confectioners' sugar until frosting reaches spreading consistency. Frost cake. **Yield:** 16-18 servings.

SQUASH AND POTATOES

Lillian Child, Omaha, Nebraska

(PICTURED ON PAGE 20)

My German grandmother taught me to cook, and she used bacon drippings in almost every recipe, even cookies! I happened upon this concoction one summer Sunday afternoon when our neighbors gave us a bumper crop of vegetables from their garden. Naturally I started with grandmother's favorite ingredient...bacon!

> 6 bacon strips, diced
> 1 large potato, peeled and diced
> 1 small onion, diced
> 1 medium zucchini, diced
> 1 medium yellow summer squash, diced
> 1 tablespoon fresh minced dill *or* 1 teaspoon dill weed
> 1/2 teaspoon salt
> 1/8 teaspoon pepper

In large skillet, cook bacon until crisp. Remove bacon; drain, discarding all but 2 tablespoons drippings. Add potato; cook and stir until lightly browned, about 5 minutes. Add onion, zucchini and yellow squash; cook until tender, about 8 minutes. Return bacon to skillet; sprinkle with dill, salt and pepper. Cook and stir for about 1 minute. **Yield:** 4-6 servings.

BUTTERNUT SQUASH CASSEROLE

Patricia Sheffer, Seneca, Pennsylvania

(PICTURED ON PAGE 20)

This casserole is very versatile! It can be served hot today and cold tomorrow, as a main dish for meatless meals or as a side dish for a dinner party. Any way you serve it, it's scrumptious!

> 5 cups shredded butternut squash
> Juice and grated peel of 1 lemon
> 1 cup raisins
> 6 to 8 dried apricots, chopped (about 1/3 cup)
> 1 apple, cubed
> 2 cups ricotta *or* cottage cheese
> 1 egg, lightly beaten
> 3 tablespoons plain yogurt, sour cream *or* buttermilk

1 teaspoon ground cinnamon
1/8 teaspoon ground nutmeg
1/2 cup chopped walnuts

In a large bowl, toss squash with lemon juice and peel. Place half in the bottom of a greased 11-in. x 7-in. x 2-in. baking dish. Combine raisins, apricots and apple; sprinkle over squash. In a small bowl, mix cheese, egg, yogurt, cinnamon and nutmeg; spread over fruit mixture. Cover with remaining squash. Sprinkle with nuts. Cover with foil; bake at 375° for 35-40 minutes or until done. **Yield:** 10-12 servings.

ZUCCHINI HAMBURGER PIE

Eloise Swisher, Roseville, Illinois
(PICTURED ON PAGE 20)

This is a family favorite handed down from my dear aunt. It is such a hearty pie that it satisfies the appetite well. And my family has always enjoyed the idea of having pie for supper!

1/2 pound ground beef
1/4 cup minced onion
1 teaspoon salt
1/2 teaspoon garlic salt
1/2 cup diced green pepper
1 teaspoon dried oregano
1 teaspoon dried parsley flakes
1/2 cup dry bread crumbs
1/4 cup grated Parmesan cheese
1 egg, lightly beaten
Pastry for double-crust deep-dish pie (9 to 10 inches)
4 cups sliced zucchini, *divided*
2 medium tomatoes, peeled and thinly sliced

In a skillet, brown ground beef with onion, salt and garlic salt; drain well. Add green pepper, oregano, parsley, bread crumbs, Parmesan cheese and egg; mix well. Set aside. Place bottom pastry in pie plate; layer 2 cups of zucchini in crust. Cover with beef mixture. Cover with tomato slices and remaining zucchini. Place top pastry over zucchini. Cut a few slits in top to vent steam. Bake at 350° for 1 hour or until crust is lightly browned. **Yield:** 6-8 servings.

SWEET-AND-SOUR ZUCCHINI

Marian Platt, Sequim, Washington
(PICTURED ON PAGE 21)

I have made this many times for potlucks. Everyone loves it and it travels nicely, too. It's a wonderful way to use up the prolific zucchini that we all have in such abundance in the summertime.

3/4 cup sugar
1 teaspoon salt
1/2 teaspoon pepper
1/3 cup vegetable oil
2/3 cup cider vinegar
2 tablespoons white wine vinegar
5 cups thinly sliced zucchini
1 small onion, chopped
1/2 cup chopped green pepper

1/2 cup chopped celery

In a large bowl, combine first six ingredients; mix well. Stir in vegetables. Cover; refrigerate several hours or overnight. **Yield:** 6-8 servings.

ACORN SQUASH RINGS

Lina Vainauskas, Shaw Air Force Base, South Carolina

I love to fix acorn squash this way. It's pretty and impressive to serve, a tasty combination of fruit and vegetable and my favorite side dish when I make meat loaf. My husband, who was a "meat and potatoes" man when we were married, requests this dish often.

2 large acorn squash (about 1-1/2 pounds *each*)
4 tablespoons butter *or* margarine, *divided*
2 tablespoons maple syrup
1 medium onion, quartered and sliced
1 large Golden Delicious apple, cut into 1/2-inch pieces
1 large Red Delicious apple, cut into 1/2-inch pieces
1 banana, sliced
1 orange, sectioned and cut into 1-inch pieces
1/2 to 1 teaspoon curry powder
1/4 to 1/2 teaspoon pepper
1/4 teaspoon salt
2 tablespoons chopped toasted almonds

Cut ends from squash. Slice each squash crosswise into four rings; remove seeds. Place rings on a greased foil-lined baking pan. In a small saucepan, bring 2 tablespoons butter and syrup to a boil. Brush each ring with syrup mixture. Cover and bake at 350° for 30 minutes. Uncover and bake another 10-15 minutes, basting with syrup mixture. In a skillet, saute onion in remaining butter. Add apples and cook until crisp-tender, about 3 minutes. Stir in banana, orange and seasonings; heat through. Place rings on serving platter; fill centers with apple mixture. Sprinkle with almonds. **Yield:** 8 servings.

ZUCCHINI PATTIES

Annabelle Cripe, Goshen, Indiana

My sister gave me this recipe and I, in turn, have given it to many of my friends. These patties have a nice flavor and are compatible with just about any entree.

2 cups shredded zucchini
1/3 cup biscuit mix
1/2 cup shredded cheddar cheese
2 tablespoons grated onion
1/2 teaspoon dried basil
1/2 teaspoon salt
1/4 teaspoon pepper
2 eggs, lightly beaten
2 tablespoons butter *or* margarine

In a bowl, combine first seven ingredients; mix well. Stir in eggs; mix well. Shape into six patties, using about 1/4 cup of zucchini mixture for each patty. In a skillet, melt butter; cook patties for 4-5 minutes per side or until lightly browned. **Yield:** 4-6 servings.

PUMPKIN ZUCCHINI BREAD

Pat Thompson, Spokane, Washington
(PICTURED AT LEFT)

Everyone in Spokane has zucchini in summer. The people who grow it have enough for all of their friends! This is one of many ways I like to use it.

    3 eggs, lightly beaten
    2 cups sugar
    1 cup canned pumpkin
    1 cup butter *or* margarine, melted
    1 tablespoon vanilla extract
    3 cups all-purpose flour
    1 teaspoon baking soda
    1/2 teaspoon baking powder
    1/2 teaspoon salt
    1/2 teaspoon ground cinnamon
    1/2 teaspoon ground nutmeg
    1/2 teaspoon ground cloves
    1 cup shredded zucchini
    1 cup chopped walnuts

In a mixing bowl, combine eggs and sugar. Add pumpkin, butter and vanilla. Combine dry ingredients; gradually add to pumpkin mixture and mix well. Stir in zucchini and nuts. Pour into two greased and floured 9-in. x 5-in. x 3-in. loaf pans. Bake at 350° for 45-50 minutes or until breads test done. Cool in pans 10 minutes. Remove to a wire rack. **Yield:** 2 loaves.

GOLDEN SQUASH ROLLS

Dolores Diercks, Clinton, Iowa
(PICTURED AT LEFT)

These rolls are a big favorite with my family and a "must" at our holiday meals. I adapted the recipe years ago from a potato roll recipe I had, so the texture is quite similar.

    2 packages (1/4 ounce *each*) active dry yeast
    1-1/2 cups warm water (110° to 115°)
    1/3 cup sugar
    2 teaspoons salt
    2 eggs
    1 cup mashed winter squash
    7 to 7-1/2 cups all-purpose flour
    2/3 cup butter *or* margarine, melted
    2 tablespoons butter *or* margarine, softened

In a large mixing bowl, dissolve yeast in water; let stand 5 minutes. Add sugar, salt, eggs, squash and 3-1/2 cups flour; beat well. Beat in melted butter. By hand, gradually add enough remaining flour to form a soft dough. Turn onto a floured board; knead until smooth and elastic, about 6-8 minutes. Place in a greased bowl, turning once to grease

BAKED GOODS. *Pictured at left, clockwise from the top: Pumpkin Zucchini Bread, Golden Squash Rolls and Chocolate Zucchini Cake (all recipes on this page).*

top. Cover and refrigerate 2-4 hours. (May refrigerate up to 3 days). Punch dough down; turn onto a floured board. Divide dough in half; roll each into a 16-in. circle; spread with softened butter. Cut each circle into 16 wedges. Roll up from wide end and place with pointed end down on greased baking sheets. Cover and let rise until almost doubled, about 1 hour. Bake at 400° for 15-20 minutes or until golden brown. **Yield:** 2-1/2 to 3 dozen.

CHOCOLATE ZUCCHINI CAKE

Eloise Swisher, Roseville, Illinois
(PICTURED AT LEFT)

The hint of chocolate in this moist cake is an unexpected flavor and a nice surprise.

    1/2 cup butter *or* margarine, softened
    1/2 cup vegetable oil
    1-1/2 cups sugar
    2 eggs, lightly beaten
    1/2 cup sour milk *or* buttermilk
    1 teaspoon vanilla extract
    2-1/2 cups all-purpose flour
    1/4 cup baking cocoa
    1 teaspoon baking soda
    1/2 teaspoon baking powder
    1/2 teaspoon salt
    1/2 teaspoon ground cinnamon
    1/4 teaspoon ground cloves
    2 cups shredded zucchini
    1/2 cup chopped nuts
    1/2 cup semisweet chocolate chips

In a mixing bowl, cream butter, oil and sugar. Add eggs, milk and vanilla; mix well. Combine flour, cocoa, baking soda, baking powder, salt, cinnamon and cloves; gradually add to creamed mixture. Stir in zucchini. Spread into a greased 13-in. x 9-in. x 2-in. baking pan. Sprinkle with nuts and chocolate chips. Bake at 350° for 35-40 minutes or until cake tests done. **Yield:** 12-16 servings.

ZUCCHINI SPREAD

Judithan Williamson, Center Harbor, New Hampshire

We entertain a lot and I always like to do something different. All our friends like this spread.

    1 cup finely shredded zucchini
    1 cup (4 ounces) shredded sharp cheddar cheese
    1/2 cup chopped walnuts
    1 teaspoon lemon juice
    3/4 cup mayonnaise
    1/2 teaspoon salt
    1/4 teaspoon pepper

Place zucchini in cheesecloth or a strainer; squeeze out excess moisture. In a bowl, combine zucchini with remaining ingredients; mix well. Cover and refrigerate at least 1 hour or overnight. Serve with crackers or raw vegetables. **Yield:** about 2 cups.

CORN

These sweet succulent kernels bring versatility to your cooking, because corn makes a wonderful addition to soups, salads, side dishes and even desserts. Try these recipes and you'll see!

CAZUELA
Louise Schmid, Marshall, Minnesota
(PICTURED AT LEFT)

I learned to make Cazuela while we were living in Chile for a few months. We grow extra butternut squash in our garden just for this favorite recipe. Besides gardening, my retired husband and I also enjoy birdwatching, volunteer work, and visting our five children and six grandchildren.

6 chicken drumsticks *or* thighs
Butternut squash, peeled and cut into 24 cubes
  (1 inch *each*)
6 small potatoes, peeled
6 pieces of corn on the cob (2 inches *each*)
3 carrots, cut into 1-inch chunks
4 cans (10-3/4 ounces *each*) chicken broth
Cooked rice
Hot pepper sauce to taste
Salt and pepper to taste
Minced fresh cilantro *or* parsley

In a large soup kettle or Dutch oven, place chicken, squash, potatoes, corn, carrots and broth; bring to a boil. Reduce heat; cover and simmer for 25 minutes or until chicken is done and vegetables are tender. Serve over rice in a shallow soup bowl; pass hot pepper sauce, salt, pepper and cilantro or parsley. **Yield:** 6-8 servings.

COUNTRY CORNCAKES
Anne Frederick, New Hartford, New York

Although we live in a suburban area, we are lucky to have plenty of farms nearby where we can purchase fresh home-grown corn. When it's out of season, though, I do substitute canned or frozen corn in this favorite recipe.

1-1/2 cups yellow cornmeal
1/4 cup all-purpose flour
1 tablespoon sugar
1 teaspoon baking soda
1/2 teaspoon salt
1 egg
1-1/2 cups buttermilk

GOLDEN GOODNESS. *Pictured at left: Cazuela (recipe above).*

2 tablespoons butter *or* margarine, melted
1-1/2 cups fresh corn
Sour cream, optional
6 bacon strips, cooked and crumbled, optional
2 tablespoons snipped fresh chives, optional

Combine the first five ingredients in a mixing bowl; make a well in the center. In another bowl, beat egg, buttermilk and butter; pour into well and stir just until blended. Gently stir in corn; do not overmix. Cover and let stand for 5 minutes. Pour batter by 1/4 cupfuls onto a lightly greased hot griddle. Turn when bubbles form on top, about 2-3 minutes. Cook until golden, about 2 minutes longer. Top with sour cream, bacon and chives if desired. **Yield:** 14 corncakes.

CORN CHOWDER
Marci Ingram, Omaha, Nebraska

Here in the "Cornhusker State", we make lots of dishes with corn! Even my kids love this soup, I've discovered. Although we live in the city, we love to spend time at my parents' cabin on a lake surrounded by farms and cornfields.

6 ears fresh corn
Milk
1 small onion, chopped
1 small green pepper, chopped
1 celery rib, chopped
1 jalapeno pepper, seeded and chopped
1 tablespoon cooking oil
3 tomatoes, peeled and chopped
2 potatoes, peeled and chopped
1 bay leaf
1 teaspoon salt
1/4 teaspoon pepper
1/4 teaspoon sugar
1/8 teaspoon ground allspice
2 cups light cream
Additional pepper, optional
Chopped fresh parsley, optional
6 bacon strips, cooked and crumbled, optional

Cut corn off cob (you'll need about 3-1/2 cups for this recipe). Rub the edge of a knife over each cob to "milk" it; add enough milk to cob juice to equal 1 cup. Set corn and liquid aside. In a large saucepan, saute onion, green pepper, celery and jalapeno in oil until soft. Add tomatoes, potatoes, bay leaf, salt, pepper, sugar and allspice; bring to a boil. Reduce heat; add cream, and the reserved corn and milk mixture. Simmer for 30-40 minutes. Garnish with parsley, pepper and bacon if desired. **Yield:** 6-8 servings (2 quarts).

"HOT" CORN BREAD
Veva Martsolf, Butler, Pennsylvania

I first tasted this bread when we visited some good friends in Arkansas in the early '70's. I have made it on many occasions since then, particularly for card club and church functions. I enjoy my job as postal clerk at our local office, and spending time with our two children and five grandchildren.

　2 eggs
　1 cup buttermilk
　1 cup homemade cream-style corn (see recipe below)
　1/2 cup vegetable oil
　1 cup (4 ounces) shredded cheddar *or* longhorn
　　cheese
　1 to 2 jalapeno peppers, chopped
　1 cup yellow cornmeal
　1/2 teaspoon baking soda
　1/2 teaspoon salt

In a mixing bowl, beat eggs. Add buttermilk, corn, oil, cheese and peppers. Combine cornmeal, baking soda and salt; stir into egg mixture. Pour into a greased 13-in. x 9-in. x 2-in. baking pan. Bake at 350° for 30 minutes. **Yield:** 16-20 servings.

CREAM-STYLE CORN
Vivian Gouliquer, Vanderhoof, British Columbia

I was raised on a farm in this small rural community. Although I'm not living on a farm at present, I'm still a country girl at heart! When I shared some fresh corn with a neighbor, she shared this recipe with me...I've found it's the best way to retain the corn's crisp sweet flavor after freezing.

　18 cups fresh corn, *divided*
　2 cups milk
　1 tablespoon pickling salt
　1/2 cup butter *or* margarine
　1/3 cup sugar

In a food processor, process half of the corn until creamy. Combine with remaining ingredients in a large baking pan. Cover and bake at 325° for 1 hour and 30 minutes, stirring frequently. **Yield:** 2 quarts. *Editor's Note:* Use this recipe in the "Hot" Corn Bread, Sage Corn Muffins and Zesty Corn Custard on this page.

ZESTY CORN CUSTARD
Joni Schaper, Lancaster, California

My mother handed this recipe down to me—I don't know what else I can say about it except that it's wonderful!

　2 cups homemade cream-style corn (see recipe
　　above)
　2 cups tomato juice
　3 eggs, beaten
　1 cup evaporated milk
　1 cup (4 ounces) shredded cheddar cheese

　1 cup yellow cornmeal
　1/2 cup finely chopped onion
　1/2 cup finely chopped green pepper
　1 teaspoon salt
　1/4 teaspoon pepper
Hot pepper sauce to taste

Combine all ingredients in a large bowl; mix thoroughly. Pour into a greased 13-in. x 9-in. x 2-in. baking dish or 2-1/2-qt. casserole. Set in a shallow pan of hot water. Bake at 350° for 50-55 minutes or until set. **Yield:** 10-12 servings.

BOSTON BAKED CORN
Mrs. Willard Wilson, Woodsfield, Ohio

My family enjoys this recipe, which I received from my sister-in-law. It's a nice side dish with many meals.

　1 cup ketchup
　2 tablespoons brown sugar
　1 teaspoon dry mustard
　1/2 teaspoon salt
　1 small onion, chopped
　3 cups fresh corn
　3 bacon strips, diced

Combine ketchup, brown sugar, mustard and salt in a bowl; stir in onion and corn and mix thoroughly. Pour into a greased 1-1/2-qt. casserole. Top with bacon. Bake, uncovered, at 350° for 40 minutes or until bacon is cooked and dish is heated through. **Yield:** 6-8 servings.

SAGE CORN MUFFINS
Velma Martin, Stirum, North Dakota

These muffins are moist and flavorful—try them instead of rolls with most any meal.

　1-1/2 cups yellow cornmeal
　1/2 cup all-purpose flour
　3 tablespoons sugar
　1 tablespoon baking powder
　1/2 teaspoon salt
　2 eggs
　1 cup buttermilk
　1/4 cup butter *or* margarine, melted
　1-1/2 cups homemade cream-style corn (see recipe
　　at left)
　1/2 cup chopped fresh sage *or* 1 to 2 teaspoons
　　ground sage
　1/4 teaspoon pepper

In a mixing bowl, combine cornmeal, flour, sugar, baking powder and salt. In another bowl, lightly beat eggs. Add buttermilk and butter; stir into dry ingredients just until combined. Fold in corn, sage and pepper. Fill 12 greased muffin cups almost to the top. Bake at 400° for 22-25 minutes or until muffins are golden and test done. **Yield:** 1 dozen.

CORN RELISH
Sherri Seifer, Paxton, Nebraska

I like to make a double batch of this relish in the fall when fresh corn's available so it lasts all winter. Try it on hamburgers, hot dogs and in potato salad—it really perks them up! My husband and I ranch in the Sandhills of Nebraska with our 2-year-old daughter—soon I'll have a helper in the kitchen!

     8 cups fresh corn
 3-1/2 cups shredded cabbage
 1-1/2 cups chopped onion
     1 cup chopped celery
   1/2 cup chopped green pepper
   1/2 cup chopped sweet red pepper
 3-1/2 cups vinegar
     2 cups water
     2 cups sugar
     2 tablespoons dry mustard
     1 tablespoon ground turmeric
     1 tablespoon mustard seed
     1 tablespoon celery seed
     1 tablespoon salt

Combine all ingredients in a Dutch oven. Bring to a boil over medium heat. Reduce heat; simmer for 20 minutes. Pour hot into hot jars, leaving 1/4-in. headspace. Adjust caps. Process for 15 minutes in a boiling-water bath. **Yield:** 6-7 pints.

PATIO SALAD
Naoma Peterson, Huron, South Dakota

My family loves this salad served with barbecued chicken or hamburgers. It's a nice change from potato salad.

   1/2 cup sour cream
   1/3 cup mayonnaise *or* salad dressing
     2 tablespoons vinegar
     1 tablespoon sugar
   1/2 teaspoon dry mustard
   1/4 teaspoon salt
     4 cups fresh corn, cooked
     1 cup diced celery
     1 cup diced unpeeled cucumber
     2 tomatoes, seeded and diced
   1/2 cup chopped onion

TO COOK FRESH CORN: *Plunge husked ears into a large kettle of boiling water. Don't salt during cooking, since salt can harden kernels. Boil until tender, about 8 to 10 minutes; less for just-picked corn.*

In a small bowl, combine sour cream, mayonnaise, vinegar, sugar, mustard and salt; set aside. In a large bowl, combine corn, celery, cucumber, tomatoes and onion. Add dressing and toss lightly. Cover and chill until ready to serve. **Yield:** 8-10 servings.

ROASTED CORN AND AVOCADO DIP
Vivian Davis, Kerrville, Texas

The tangy taste of this dip keeps people who taste it guessing what's in it! I've had many people request the recipe to find out. My husband and I enjoy traveling in our motor home and doing a little fishing along the way.

     1 cup fresh corn
     2 tablespoons vegetable oil
     2 large avocados, peeled
     3 tablespoons lime juice
     2 garlic cloves, minced
     2 tablespoons minced onion
     1 can (3-1/2 ounces) jalapeno peppers, drained and chopped
   1/2 teaspoon salt
   1/4 teaspoon ground cumin
Tortilla chips

Combine corn and oil in a shallow baking dish. Bake at 400° for 12-15 minutes or until lightly browned, stirring several times. Cool. Meanwhile, chop 1 avocado and set aside. Mash the other avocado in a bowl; add lime juice, garlic, onion, jalapenos, salt and cumin. Fold in chopped avocado and the corn. Chill. Serve with tortilla chips. **Yield:** 2-1/2 cups.

CORN COBBLER
Vivian Hippert, Richland, Pennsylvania

While thinking of a shortcut for what we Pennsylvania Dutch call "Corn Pie", I thought of using biscuit mix instead of pie dough. I tried my version on some friends who were visiting, and they scraped the dish clean!

     2 cups diced peeled potatoes
   1/2 cup chopped onion
 1-1/2 teaspoons salt
   1/2 teaspoon pepper
     2 cups water
     4 cups fresh corn
 2-3/4 cups milk, *divided*
   1/4 cup sliced green onions
     2 tablespoons minced fresh parsley
     6 hard-cooked eggs, sliced
     3 cups biscuit mix

Place potatoes, onion, salt, pepper and water in a large saucepan. Bring to a boil and boil, uncovered, for 5 minutes. Add corn; return to boiling and boil for 2 minutes. Drain. Add 1-3/4 cups milk, green onions and parsley. Pour into a greased 13-in. x 9-in. x 2-in. baking dish. Top with eggs. Mix biscuit mix and remaining milk until smooth; drop by teaspoonfuls onto corn mixture. Bake at 450° for 13-15 minutes or until done. **Yield:** 6-8 servings.

COLORFUL KERNELS. *Clockwise from lower left: Enchilada Casserole, Herb Butter for Corn, Fiesta Corn Salad, Red Corn Relish and Down-Home Succotash (all recipes on pages 32 and 33).*

DOWN-HOME SUCCOTASH
Marian Platt, Sequim, Washington
(PICTURED ON PAGE 31)

If you grow your own corn, you can have it be really fresh for this recipe if you make sure everything is ready before you pick the corn! That's the way I like it.

　1/4 pound sliced bacon, chopped
　　2 cups fresh corn
　1/2 pound lima beans
　　1 medium green pepper, chopped
　　1 medium onion, chopped
　　2 medium tomatoes, cut into wedges

In a skillet, cook bacon until crisp. Remove bacon to paper towels and drain all but 1 tablespoon drippings. To skillet, add corn, beans, green pepper and onion. Simmer for 10-15 minutes or until vegetables are almost tender, adding water if necessary. Stir in tomatoes and bacon; cook just until tomatoes are heated through. **Yield:** 12-14 servings.

FIESTA CORN SALAD
Marian Platt, Sequim, Washington
(PICTURED ON PAGE 30)

This salad is great for potlucks since it travels well and goes with everything. Have you heard the old wives' tale about planting corn? It says if you laugh when planting corn, it won't grow as high as you'd like!

　　2 cups fresh corn, cooked
　　3 tomatoes, chopped
　　1 can (2-1/4 ounces) sliced pitted ripe olives, drained
　1/4 cup sliced green olives
　　2 tablespoons taco seasoning mix
　1/4 cup vegetable oil
　1/4 cup vinegar
　1/4 cup water

In a large bowl, combine corn, tomatoes and olives. In a small bowl, combine seasoning mix, oil, vinegar and water; pour over corn mixture and mix well. Chill several hours before serving. **Yield:** 8-10 servings.

RED CORN RELISH
Belva Parker, Viroqua, Wisconsin
(PICTURED ON PAGE 31)

I discovered this recipe years ago and found it a great way to utilize the last of the garden produce. It tastes good with any meat during the long winter months. A pint didn't last long in our family of six girls, who are all married now.

4-1/2 cups fresh corn
　　3 large onions, chopped
　　1 sweet red pepper, chopped
　　1 green pepper, chopped
　　3 large cucumbers, seeded and chopped

　　3 cups shredded cabbage
　　4 pounds tomatoes, peeled and chopped
　　2 cups sugar
1-1/2 cups vinegar
　1/4 cup salt
　　1 tablespoon celery seed
　　1 tablespoon mustard seed
1-1/2 teaspoons ground turmeric

Combine all ingredients in a large Dutch oven. Bring to a boil over medium heat, stirring occasionally. Reduce heat; simmer, uncovered, for 40 minutes or until vegetables are tender and mixture has thickened. Pack hot into hot jars, leaving 1/4-in. headspace. Adjust caps. Process for 15 minutes in a boiling-water bath. **Yield:** about 10 pints.

HERB BUTTER FOR CORN
Ellen Bower, Taneytown, Maryland
(PICTURED ON PAGE 30)

This is a sweet treat for corn on the cob, especially tasty on corn done on the grill. It's a nice change from plain butter—and easier than sprinkling seasonings separately!

　　1 cup butter *or* margarine, softened
　　1 teaspoon chopped fresh sweet basil *or* 1/2 teaspoon dried basil

In a small bowl, combine butter and basil until smooth. Spread on cooked corn on the cob. Refrigerate leftovers.

CORNY TURKEY BURGERS
Audrey Thibodeau, Fountain Hills, Arizona

If you like spicy food, you'll love these burgers! When I added the jalapeno pepper to my regular turkey burgers and served them with the sauce, they were a hit. You can also grill them.

BURGERS:
　　1 pound ground turkey
　1/4 cup yellow cornmeal
　　1 egg, lightly beaten
　1/2 to 1 jalapeno pepper, seeded and chopped
　　1 tablespoon lime juice
　　2 to 4 drops hot pepper sauce
　1/2 to 1 teaspoon ground cumin
　1/4 teaspoon salt
　1/8 teaspoon pepper
　　2 tablespoons cooking oil
SAUCE:
　　1 cup fresh corn, cooked
　　1 cup picante sauce
　　1 tablespoon lime juice

In a medium bowl, combine the first nine ingredients; mix well. Shape into four patties. Heat oil in skillet; fry patties over medium heat for about 4 minutes per side or until done. Heat sauce ingredients in a small saucepan; serve over burgers. Serve on hamburger buns if desired. **Yield:** 4 servings.

ENCHILADA CASSEROLE

Nancy VanderVeer, Knoxville, Iowa

(PICTURED ON PAGE 30)

I get great reviews every time I serve this—even from my father who usually doesn't like Mexican food. My husband and I have two children and I enjoy cooking, cross-stitching and painting.

> 1 pound ground beef
> 1 can (10 ounces) enchilada sauce
> 1 cup salsa
> 6 flour tortillas (10 inch)
> 2 cups fresh corn
> 4 cups (16 ounces) shredded cheddar cheese

In a skillet, brown ground beef; drain. Stir in enchilada sauce and salsa; set aside. Place two tortillas, overlapping as necessary, in the bottom of a greased 13-in. x 9-in. x 2-in. baking dish. Cover with one-third of the meat mixture; top with 1 cup corn; sprinkle with 1-1/3 cups cheese. Repeat layers once, then top with remaining tortillas, meat and cheese. Bake, uncovered, at 350° for 30 minutes or until bubbly. **Yield:** 6-8 servings.

CORN WITH BASIL

Ronda Lambert, Vandervoort, Arkansas

Our family enjoys eating lots of corn fresh from our garden. Along with the garden, my husband and I and our five children raise chickens and cows on our farm.

> 3-1/2 cups fresh corn
> 1 medium onion, chopped
> 1/2 cup thinly sliced celery
> 1 garlic clove, minced
> 2 tablespoons butter *or* margarine
> 1 jar (2 ounces) diced pimientos, drained, optional
> 1 teaspoon dried basil
> 1/2 teaspoon salt

In a skillet over medium heat, cook and stir corn, onion, celery and garlic in butter for 10 minutes. Stir in pimientos, basil and salt; cover and simmer, stirring often, for 15-20 minutes or until corn is tender. **Yield:** 4-6 servings.

SAUSAGE CORN CHOWDER

Sharon Wallace, Omaha, Nebraska

This hearty soup is a meal in itself when served with a salad and bread. For a spicier flavor, I sometimes substitute Mexicorn for the whole kernel corn.

> 2 packages (7 ounces *each*) pork *or* turkey breakfast sausage
> 2 cans (10-3/4 ounces *each*) condensed cream of chicken soup, undiluted

2-1/2 cups milk
> 2 cups fresh corn
> 2/3 cup sliced green onions
> 1/2 teaspoon hot pepper sauce
> 1 cup (4 ounces) shredded Swiss cheese

Crumble sausage into a large saucepan or Dutch oven; brown over medium heat. Drain. Add soup, milk, corn, green onions and hot pepper sauce. Cook until corn is tender. Reduce heat to low; add cheese and heat until melted. **Yield:** 6-8 servings (2 quarts).

SUCCOTASH SALAD

Bonnie Baumgardner, Sylva, North Carolina

You'll have the chance to use several garden-fresh vegetables in this recipe, which is a "spiced-up" version of regular succotash.

> 2-1/2 cups fresh corn, cooked and cooled
> 1 package (10 ounces) frozen lima beans, cooked, drained and cooled
> 4 ounces Monterey Jack cheese, cubed
> 2 medium radishes, chopped
> 2 medium tomatoes, seeded and chopped
> 2 celery ribs, diced
> 1 small onion, chopped
> 1/4 cup vegetable oil
> 3 tablespoons white wine vinegar
> 3/4 teaspoon ground cumin
> 1/2 teaspoon salt
> 1/2 teaspoon pepper

In a large bowl, combine corn, beans, cheese, radishes, tomatoes, celery and onion. Mix remaining ingredients in a small bowl; pour over vegetables and toss to coat. Refrigerate for 2-3 hours before serving. **Yield:** 10-12 servings.

FRESH VEGETABLE KABOBS

Suzanne McKinley, Lyons, Georgia

These are quick and easy to prepare, and a fun way to eat vegetables—our kids love them! We like to put the kabobs on the grill, which we do a lot of in summer to keep from heating up the kitchen.

> 2 medium ears fresh corn, cut into 2-inch pieces
> 2 medium zucchini, cut into 1-inch pieces
> 8 boiling onions *or* 1 package (8 ounces) boiling onions, cooked
> 1/2 cup butter *or* margarine, melted
> 2 tablespoons minced fresh chives
> 2 tablespoons minced fresh parsley
> 1/2 teaspoon garlic salt

Thread the corn, zucchini and onions alternately on four large skewers. Combine butter, chives, parsley and garlic salt; mix well. Place skewers on a broiler pan; broil for about 8-10 minutes, turning and brushing with butter mixture every 2 minutes. **Yield:** 4 servings.

CORN-STUFFED PEPPERS

Suzanne Hubbard, Greeley, Colorado

(PICTURED AT RIGHT)

I created this recipe—and haven't had any complaints yet! The peppers can be served alone as a meal or alongside pork chops, steak, hamburgers, etc. I love to cook...outside the kitchen, I enjoy crafts and writing.

　4 medium green peppers
　1 can (10-3/4 ounces) condensed cream of celery
　　soup, undiluted
2-1/2 cups frozen loose-pack hash browns, thawed
　2 cups fresh corn, cooked
　1/2 cup shredded cheddar cheese
　1/4 cup chopped onion
　1 jar (2 ounces) chopped pimientos, drained
　2 tablespoons snipped fresh chives
　1/2 teaspoon salt

Slice tops off peppers and reserve; remove seeds. In a bowl, combine the remaining ingredients. Spoon filling into peppers and replace tops. Place in an 8-in. square baking dish; cover with foil. Bake at 350° for 45-60 minutes. **Yield:** 4 servings.

"IOWA IN A BOWL"

Clara Eaves, Waterloo, Iowa

After I tasted this salad at a church picnic, I had to get the recipe. It's a delicious way to serve corn—everyone I've ever served it to has loved it!

　3 cups fresh corn, cooked
　3 green onions, sliced
　2 small tomatoes, diced
　3/4 cup diced unpeeled cucumber
　1/4 cup diced onion
　1/4 cup sour cream
　2 tablespoons mayonnaise
　1 tablespoon white vinegar
　1 teaspoon sugar
　1/2 teaspoon salt
　1/4 teaspoon celery seed
　1/4 teaspoon dry mustard

In a large bowl, combine corn, green onions, tomatoes, cucumber and onion. Combine remaining ingredients in a small bowl; pour over vegetables and toss to coat. Cover and refrigerate for several hours or overnight. **Yield:** 8-10 servings.

CORN HILL CORN BREAD

Ellen Burr, Truro, Massachusetts

I named this recipe after the wooded hill that we can see from our house. It is said that the Pilgrims discovered a cache of Indian corn here in Truro, near the tip of Cape Cod, that enabled them to survive their first harsh winter in the New World.

1-1/4 cups all-purpose flour
　3/4 cup yellow cornmeal
　1/3 cup sugar
　2 teaspoons baking powder
　1/2 teaspoon salt
　1/2 teaspoon ground coriander
　1/2 teaspoon ground ginger
　1/2 teaspoon dried thyme
　1/8 teaspoon ground mace
　1 egg
　1 cup milk
　1/4 cup vegetable oil
　1 cup fresh corn, cooked
　2 teaspoons cinnamon-sugar

In a large bowl, combine flour, cornmeal, sugar, baking powder, salt, coriander, ginger, thyme and mace. In a small bowl, lightly beat egg. Add milk and oil; stir into dry ingredients just until combined. Fold in corn. Pour into a greased 8-in. square baking pan. Sprinkle with cinnamon-sugar. Bake at 400° for 20-25 minutes or until done. **Yield:** 9 servings.

TACO SOUP

Nancy Wilkes, Preston, Idaho

(PICTURED AT RIGHT)

If you need a meal in a hurry, this fast recipe fills the bill! When I have time, I like to make "edible bowls" of bread to serve the soup in—it makes for a unique presentation and a hearty main dish!

　1 pound ground beef
　1/4 cup chopped onion
　2 cups fresh corn
　1 can (16 ounces) tomatoes with liquid, cut up
　1 can (15-1/2 ounces) kidney beans, rinsed and
　　drained
　1 can (8 ounces) tomato sauce
　1 envelope (1-1/4 ounces) taco seasoning
Corn chips, shredded cheddar cheese *and/or* sour cream,
　optional

In a large saucepan, brown ground beef and onion; drain. Add corn, tomatoes, kidney beans, tomato sauce and taco seasoning. Cover and simmer for 15 minutes, stirring occasionally. Serve with corn chips, cheese and/or sour cream if desired. **Yield:** 4-6 servings (1-1/2 quarts).

CORN MEALS. *Pictured at right: Corn-Stuffed Peppers and Taco Soup (recipes above).*

CORN SLAW
Sue Burton, Frankfort, Kansas

My mother gave this recipe to me. It's one my husband and two daughters ask for often in summer, especially when we're having a grilled meal.

2 cups fresh corn, cooked
1 cup diced carrots
1 cup diced green pepper
1/2 cup chopped onion
1/4 cup mayonnaise
1/4 cup sour cream
2 teaspoons vinegar
1 teaspoon sugar
1 teaspoon prepared yellow mustard
1/4 teaspoon salt

In a salad bowl, toss corn, carrots, green pepper and onion. In a small bowl, combine remaining ingredients; pour over vegetables and mix well. Refrigerate for several hours before serving. **Yield:** 8 servings.

MEXICAN FRIED CORN
Sylvia Kessick, Dewey, Arizona

When I was growing up, my mother used to serve fried corn for breakfast with scrambled eggs and tortillas. Here in Arizona, corn is widely used in many dishes. This is a great way to use it—my husband and I both enjoy it.

3 cups fresh corn
1/2 cup diced onion
1/4 cup butter *or* margarine
1 can (4 ounces) chopped green chilies
Salt and pepper to taste

In a skillet, cook corn and onion in butter until tender. Add chilies, salt and pepper; cook and stir over medium heat for about 5-7 minutes. Serve immediately. **Yield:** 4-6 servings.

CORN AND SPINACH SOUFFLE
Rebecca Miller, St. Cloud, Minnesota

This is an easy, foolproof souffle—you just need to make sure the vegetables and sauce are cool before adding the eggs. I've made this many times for guests and always receive compliments, even from people who don't like spinach.

1-3/4 cups fresh corn, cooked
1-1/4 cups chopped cooked spinach (well drained)
1/4 cup butter *or* margarine
2 tablespoons all-purpose flour
1-1/2 teaspoons salt
3/4 cup evaporated milk
3 eggs, lightly beaten
1 tablespoon chopped pimientos
2 teaspoons dried minced onion

Combine corn and spinach; set aside. In a saucepan over

low heat, melt butter. Add flour and stir to make a smooth paste. Stir in salt. Gradually add milk; cook, stirring constantly, until thickened. Cool. Combine eggs, pimientos and onion; fold into cooled butter mixture. Fold in corn and spinach. Pour into a greased 8-1/2-in. x 4-3/8-in. x 2-1/2-in. loaf pan. Bake at 350° for 45-50 minutes or until done. Slice to serve. **Yield:** 8 servings.

CORN 'N' CUCUMBERS
Jean Moore, Pliny, West Virginia

This was one of my mother's recipes and I think of her whenever I make it. It's a nice change from a regular cucumber salad.

2 medium cucumbers, peeled and thinly sliced
2 cups fresh corn, cooked
1/2 medium onion, thinly sliced
1/2 cup vinegar
2 tablespoons sugar
2 tablespoons water
1 teaspoon dill weed
1 teaspoon salt
1/4 teaspoon pepper
Pinch cayenne pepper

Combine all ingredients in a large bowl. Cover and chill for several hours. **Yield:** 8-10 servings.

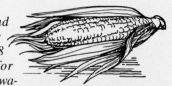

TO FREEZE FRESH CORN: *Husk ears and remove silk. Blanch ears in boiling water for 8 minutes; 10 minutes for large ears. Chill in cold water. Package in moisture-proof wrapping. For kernel corn, blanch 4-1/2 minutes. Cut off kernels and cool as above. Pack tightly to remove air spaces in freezer bags or jars.*

MEXI-CORN LASAGNA
Darlene Clayton, Danbury, Wisconsin

Tortillas and a spicy meat sauce plus the corn make this lasagna out of the ordinary! I like to serve it with a salad and corn bread.

1 pound ground beef
2 cups fresh corn
1 can (15 ounces) tomato sauce
1 cup picante sauce
1 tablespoon chili powder
1-1/2 teaspoons ground cumin
10 flour tortillas (7 inch)
2 cups cottage cheese
2 eggs, lightly beaten
1/4 cup grated Parmesan cheese
1 teaspoon dried oregano
1/2 teaspoon garlic salt
1 cup (4 ounces) shredded cheddar cheese

In a skillet, brown ground beef. Drain. Add corn, tomato sauce, picante sauce, chili powder and cumin; bring to a boil. Reduce heat; cover and simmer for 5 minutes. Place half of the tortillas in the bottom and up the sides of a greased 13-in. x 9-in. x 2-in. baking pan. Spoon meat mixture over tortillas. Combine cottage cheese, eggs, Parmesan, oregano and garlic salt; spread over meat mixture. Top with remaining tortillas. Cover with foil. Bake at 375° for 30 minutes. Sprinkle with cheese; return to the oven for 10 minutes or until cheese is melted. **Yield:** 12 servings.

CORN VEGETABLE CASSEROLE
Roy and Jerretta Logan, Ferguson, Missouri

This casserole is great for a potluck or anytime you need to make a dish ahead of time, then bake before serving. Corn is a favorite at our house—when we had this at Thanksgiving, it was a big hit.

3-1/2 cups fresh corn
   3 cups chopped broccoli, parboiled
   2 cups sliced carrots (1/2-inch pieces), parboiled
1-1/2 cups pearl onions
   1 can (10-3/4 ounces) condensed cream of corn soup, undiluted
   1/2 cup milk
   1 tablespoon Worcestershire sauce
   1 teaspoon garlic powder
1-1/2 cups (6 ounces) shredded cheddar cheese, *divided*

Combine corn, broccoli, carrots and onions; place in a greased 13-in. x 9-in. x 2-in. baking dish. In a bowl, combine soup, milk, Worcestershire sauce and garlic powder. Add 1 cup cheese. Pour over vegetables. Top with remaining cheese. Bake at 350° for 35-40 minutes or until bubbly and heated through. **Yield:** 12 servings.

DOUBLE CORN BAKE
Janie Hutchison, Walker, Missouri

I plant a big garden, which includes a lot of corn. My seven grandchildren enjoy coming to help pick and husk the corn. When our family gets together, they tell me "bring corn".

   1 pound ground beef
1/3 cup chopped onion
1/3 cup ketchup
1/2 teaspoon salt
1/2 teaspoon chili powder
1/4 teaspoon dried oregano
1-1/2 cups fresh corn, cooked
   1 package (8-1/2 ounces) corn bread mix
   3 tablespoons butter *or* margarine, melted, *divided*
   1 can (16 ounces) tomatoes with liquid, cut up
   1 tablespoon cornstarch

In a skillet, brown beef with onion. Drain. Add ketchup, salt, chili powder and oregano; cook for 5 minutes. Cool slightly. With a spoon, press meat mixture into the bottom and up the sides of a greased 10-in. pie plate. Spoon corn into crust. Prepare corn bread batter according to package di-

rections; stir in 2 tablespoons melted butter. Spread over corn. Bake at 425° for 20 minutes. Meanwhile, combine tomatoes, cornstarch and remaining butter in a saucepan; cook and stir for 5-10 minutes or until thickened. Cut pie into wedges and serve with sauce. **Yield:** 6-8 servings.

CORN MEDLEY
Deborah Shoupe, Cincinnati, Ohio

Cooking with corn brings back memories for me...my family grew corn on the farm where I grew up in North Carolina. I remember picking up corn the picker left behind in fall. This recipe is a colorful side dish for anyone who loves vegetables.

1/4 cup butter *or* margarine
1/4 cup chopped onion
4-1/2 cups diced peeled yellow summer squash (about 4 squash)
   3 cups fresh corn
   3 large tomatoes, peeled and diced
1-1/4 teaspoons salt
1/4 teaspoon pepper

Melt butter in a large saucepan over medium heat. Saute onion until soft, about 3-5 minutes. Add remaining ingredients; bring to a boil. Reduce heat; cover and simmer for 10-15 minutes or until vegetables are done. **Yield:** 10 servings.

SPICY CORN AND BLACK BEAN RELISH
Gail Segreto, Elizabeth, Colorado

This relish can be served as a salad or garnish with a Southwestern meal—it's especially good with chicken.

2-1/2 cups fresh corn, cooked
   1 can (15 ounces) black beans, rinsed and drained
   3/4 to 1 cup chopped seeded anaheim chili peppers
1/8 to 1/4 cup chopped seeded jalapeno peppers
1/4 cup vinegar
   2 tablespoons vegetable oil
   1 tablespoon Dijon mustard
   1 teaspoon chili powder
   1 teaspoon ground cumin
3/4 teaspoon salt
1/2 teaspoon pepper

In a large bowl, combine corn, beans and peppers. Combine remaining ingredients in a small bowl; pour over corn mixture and toss to coat. Chill. **Yield:** 6-8 servings.

POTATOES

Some may see the potato as plain...but these cooks beg to differ!
This common vegetable can be prepared in so many uncommon ways, there's
nothing plain about it. Why not dig into one of these potato dishes today?

GERMAN POTATO SALAD

Mary Fritch, Jasper, Indiana
(PICTURED AT LEFT)

This recipe has been in my family for over 100 years! At family get-togethers, it never fails to please.

12 to 14 red potatoes (about 4 pounds), cooked and
  peeled
2 hard-cooked eggs, sliced
4 bacon strips, diced
1 medium onion, chopped
2 cups water
1/2 cup vinegar
1/2 cup sugar
2 tablespoons cornstarch
4 teaspoons salt
1-1/2 teaspoons prepared mustard
1 teaspoon celery seed
1/4 teaspoon pepper

Slice potatoes into a large bowl. Add eggs; set aside. In a skillet, cook bacon and onion. Drain, reserving 3 tablespoons drippings. Add bacon and onion to potato mixture. Add remaining ingredients to the drippings; cook and stir until slightly thickened. Pour over potato mixture and toss to coat. Serve warm. **Yield:** 8-10 servings.

SWEET POTATO SALAD

Mrs. Willard Wilson, Woodsfield, Ohio

(PICTURED AT LEFT)

My mother used to make this potato salad. We all liked it back then—and now my family likes it, too!

3 pounds sweet potatoes, cooked, peeled and cubed
1/2 cup chopped onion
1 cup chopped sweet red pepper
1-1/4 cups mayonnaise
1-1/2 teaspoons salt
1/2 teaspoon pepper
1/4 teaspoon hot pepper sauce

PLEASING PICNIC POTATOES. *Pictured at left, from the top: German Potato Salad, Sweet Potato Salad, Red, White and Green Salad (all recipes on this page).*

In a large bowl, mix sweet potatoes, onion and red pepper. In a small bowl, blend remaining ingredients; add to potato mixture and toss to coat. Chill. **Yield:** 10-12 servings.

RED, WHITE AND GREEN SALAD

Jodie McCoy, Tulsa, Oklahoma
(PICTURED AT LEFT)

This is a great summertime salad—crisp, refreshing...and easy to prepare! Try it at your next family picnic.

1 pound small red potatoes, cooked and cubed
2 large tomatoes, diced
1 pound green beans, cut into 2-inch pieces and
  cooked
7 tablespoons olive oil
5 tablespoons white wine vinegar
3/4 teaspoon salt
1/2 teaspoon pepper

In a large bowl, combine potatoes, tomatoes and beans. In a small bowl, combine oil, vinegar, salt and pepper. Pour dressing over vegetables; toss to coat. Refrigerate for several hours before serving. **Yield:** 8-10 servings.

POTATO CASSEROLE

Jean Moss, Carlsbad, New Mexico

I'm lucky enough to have two daughters-in-law who are really great cooks. They have given me lots of recipes—including this one! I always take this casserole to potluck dinners.

5 to 6 medium potatoes, cooked, peeled and diced
3/4 cup butter *or* margarine, melted, *divided*
1 jar (2 ounces) chopped pimientos, drained
1/2 cup chopped green pepper
1 cup evaporated milk
1-1/2 teaspoons salt
1/4 teaspoon pepper
3/4 cup shredded cheddar cheese
24 saltine crackers, crushed (about 1 cup)

In a large bowl, combine potatoes, 1/2 cup butter, pimientos, green pepper, milk, salt, pepper and cheese. Mix thoroughly; transfer to a greased 13-in. x 9-in. x 2-in. baking dish. Sprinkle with crackers. Drizzle with remaining butter. Bake at 350° for 45 minutes. **Yield:** 10-12 servings.

BREAKFAST POTATOES

Joan Terrillion, Croghan, New York

This dish is a big hit with my family—and at the church breakfasts and brunches that I often cater. The recipe can easily be cut in half for breakfast for two...or doubled or even tripled for a crowd!

5 to 6 potatoes (about 2 pounds), cooked, peeled and cubed
1 can (10-3/4 ounces) condensed cream of mushroom soup, undiluted
1 cup (8 ounces) sour cream
1 small onion, chopped
1 small green pepper, chopped
1 cup (4 ounces) shredded cheddar cheese
2 cups cornflakes
1/4 cup butter *or* margarine, melted

In a large bowl, combine potatoes, soup, sour cream, onion, green pepper and cheese. Pour into a greased 2-1/2-qt. baking dish. Combine cornflakes and butter; sprinkle over potato mixture. Bake at 350° for 40 minutes. **Yield:** 6-8 servings.

POTATAS FORRADAS

Mary Jo Amos, Noel, Missouri

Served with eggs, salsa and refried beans, these bacon-wrapped potatoes are part of a traditional Mexican breakfast. But they're just as good with toast and a fruit cup—and they make a great side dish at dinner.

3 tablespoons butter *or* margarine, melted
Garlic salt to taste
4 medium potatoes, cooked and peeled
1/2 teaspoon dried cilantro *or* parsley flakes
Salt to taste
4 bacon strips
1 green onion, thinly sliced

In a small bowl, combine butter and garlic salt. Brush over potatoes. Sprinkle with cilantro or parsley and salt. Wrap a bacon slice around each potato; secure with a toothpick. Place in an ungreased baking dish; bake at 375° for 25-30 minutes or until bacon is crisp. Sprinkle with green onion before serving. **Yield:** 4 servings.

SHEEPHERDER'S POTATOES

Deborah Hill, Coffeyville, Kansas

Thyme adds a nice flavor surprise to this hearty casserole. Serve it as a side dish at dinner—or as the main course at breakfast or brunch.

5 to 6 medium potatoes (about 2 pounds), cooked, peeled and sliced
12 bacon strips, cooked and crumbled
1 large onion, chopped

6 eggs
1/4 cup milk
1 teaspoon salt
1/2 teaspoon pepper
2 tablespoons dried parsley flakes
1/2 teaspoon dried thyme
1/2 cup shredded cheddar cheese

In a greased 13-in. x 9-in. x 2-in. baking dish, layer potatoes, bacon and onion. In a bowl, beat eggs, milk, salt, pepper, parsley and thyme. Pour over potato mixture. Bake at 350° for 15 minutes or until eggs are almost set. Sprinkle with cheese; bake an additional 5 minutes or until cheese melts and eggs are set. **Yield:** 6-8 servings.

NEW ENGLAND FISH CHOWDER

Diane Vachon, Berwick, Maine

This is an old recipe handed down through the years. It always tasted best when made by a friend of mine who was a fisherman. There was nothing quite like sitting down with friends on a cold snowy night, enjoying this hot chowder, fresh biscuits and good conversation.

1/4 pound salt pork *or* bacon
3 onions, sliced
4 cups diced uncooked peeled potatoes
9 cups water, *divided*
2 cups milk
1 tablespoon butter *or* margarine
1-1/2 teaspoons salt
1 teaspoon pepper
2 to 3 pounds haddock fillets, cut into large chunks
Minced fresh parsley

Fry salt pork or bacon in a large soup kettle or Dutch oven. Remove and set aside. Add onions, potatoes and 5 cups of water to drippings. Cook until potatoes are tender. Add milk, butter, salt and pepper. Meanwhile, in a large saucepan, cook fish in remaining water until tender, about 10 minutes. Add fish and 2 cups of cooking liquid to potato mixture. Heat through. Garnish with parsley and salt pork or bacon. **Yield:** 16-18 servings (about 5 quarts).

SKIER'S STEW

Traci Gangwer, Denver, Colorado

This recipe is called "Skier's Stew" because you put it in the oven...and head for the slopes! It looks after itself for 5 hours. I like to prepare it two or three times a month in the fall and winter. When I come home after a busy day and get in out of the cold, a good hot dinner is waiting for me!

2 pounds beef stew meat, cut into 1-inch cubes
6 large potatoes, peeled and cut into 1-inch cubes
8 to 10 carrots, sliced
1/2 cup water
1 can (15 ounces) tomato sauce
1 envelope dry onion soup mix

In a Dutch oven, place half of the meat, potatoes and carrots. Repeat layers. Add water and tomato sauce; sprinkle onion soup mix over the top. *Do not stir.* Cover and bake at 250° for 5 hours. **Yield:** 6-8 servings.

MEXICAN TATERS AND BEANS
E. Marilyn Nix, Truth or Consequences, New Mexico

I made up this recipe and tried it out at one of the potlucks held at our church. Everyone loved it! It's grand for a group.

   6 cups sliced cooked peeled potatoes
   1 large onion, chopped
   2 cups salsa
   2 tablespoons butter *or* margarine, melted
   6 slices Monterey Jack cheese
   6 slices cheddar cheese
   2 cans (15 ounces *each*) chili with beans
   1 cup (4 ounces) shredded Monterey Jack cheese
   1 cup (4 ounces) shredded cheddar cheese
   1 cup crushed tortilla chips

Place potatoes in the bottom of a greased 13-in. x 9-in. x 2-in. baking dish. Sprinkle with onion. Mix salsa and butter; pour over onion and potatoes. Top with sliced cheeses; spread with chili. Sprinkle shredded cheeses over top. Bake at 350° for 50 minutes. Sprinkle with chips just before serving. **Yield:** 10-12 servings.

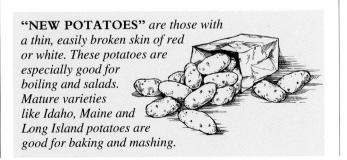

VEGETABLE PANCAKES
Agnes Landgraf, Hastings, Nebraska

I've used this recipe for more than 40 years. The pancakes are delicious with cheese sauce, creamed chipped beef or sausage gravy. Perhaps children who love pancakes but don't like vegetables would like these!

   1/2 medium onion, finely chopped
   2 medium potatoes, peeled and shredded
   3 carrots, shredded
   2 cups packed fresh spinach, sliced
   1/4 head lettuce, finely sliced
   2 eggs, lightly beaten
   1 cup all-purpose flour
   1 teaspoon baking powder

"NEW POTATOES" *are those with a thin, easily broken skin of red or white. These potatoes are especially good for boiling and salads. Mature varieties like Idaho, Maine and Long Island potatoes are good for baking and mashing.*

   1 teaspoon salt
   1/8 teaspoon pepper

In a bowl, combine all of the vegetables. Stir in eggs; mix well. Combine dry ingredients; add to vegetables. Drop batter by 1/4 cupfuls onto a hot well-oiled skillet. Spread into 4-in. circles. Cook until brown on each side. **Yield:** 4-6 servings.

CALIFORNIA POTATO SALAD
Mae Wilmoth, Anaheim, California

I clipped this recipe from the newspaper years ago and it has been a family favorite ever since. California grows many avocados, and this is my favorite way to use them.

   1 cup (8 ounces) sour cream
1-1/2 teaspoons salt
   1/2 teaspoon pepper
   1/2 teaspoon caraway seed
   1 tablespoon lemon juice
   1/4 cup chopped fresh parsley
   2 avocados, peeled and diced
   3 cups potatoes, cooked, peeled and cubed
   1/4 cup chopped onion
   8 bacon strips, cooked and crumbled, *divided*
   1 tomato, cut into wedges
Additional parsley

In a small bowl, combine sour cream, salt, pepper, caraway seed, lemon juice and parsley; set aside. In a large bowl, combine avocados, potatoes, onion and half of the bacon. Add sour cream mixture and toss lightly to coat. To serve, place salad in a large serving bowl. Arrange tomato wedges around outer edge; sprinkle with parsley and remaining bacon. **Yield:** 6-8 servings.

CHEESY POTATO CHOWDER
Carol Traxler, Philo, Illinois

This chowder was invented by my niece, who took a basic potato soup recipe and added some of her own ingredients. The results were "souperb"! I was a cook at the time, and I tried her recipe at work. It was the hit of the season!

   8 to 12 medium potatoes, peeled and cubed
   3 carrots, diced
   2 cans (14-1/2 ounces *each*) chicken broth
   1 pound process American cheese, cubed
   1 teaspoon dill weed
   1/4 teaspoon salt
   1/4 teaspoon pepper
   1/2 pound bacon, cooked and crumbled, *divided*
   3 cups milk

In a large kettle or Dutch oven, cook potatoes and carrots in chicken broth until tender, about 10 minutes. Add cheese, dill weed, salt and pepper. Cook and stir until cheese is melted. Reserve some of the bacon for ganish; add the rest to chowder with milk. Heat through. Top individual bowls with reserved bacon. **Yield:** 10-12 servings (3 quarts).

SPLENDID SPUDS! *Clockwise from top left: Ranch-Style Potato Salad, Hodgepodge Stew, Sweet Potato Bread, Au Gratin Potatoes, Potato Frittata and Spiced Potatoes (recipes on pages 44 and 45).*

RANCH-STYLE POTATO SALAD

Carol Jacobson, Covina, California
(PICTURED ON PAGE 42)

Even though I live in town, I have a feeling that this potato salad would be welcome fare at any ranch. It's a tasty, refreshing change from your typical potato salad. Serve it with pickled watermelon rinds and fresh biscuits for a great breakfast!

    1 pound bulk Italian sausage
    1 small onion, chopped
    1 large sweet red pepper, chopped
    8 medium potatoes, cooked, peeled and cubed
    6 hard-cooked eggs, chopped
    2 cups ranch-style salad dressing
    3 tablespoons minced watercress, optional

In a skillet, brown sausage; drain. Add onion and red pepper; saute until tender. Add potatoes and eggs; heat through. Add dressing and watercress if desired. **Yield:** 6-8 servings.

SPICED POTATOES

Mary Fitch, Lakewood, Colorado
(PICTURED ON PAGE 42)

Red pepper flakes give a little zip to this buttery potato dish. It's especially good with fresh fish.

    6 to 8 medium unpeeled red potatoes, sliced
    1/2 cup butter *or* margarine, melted
    1 tablespoon dried oregano
    1 garlic clove, minced
    1/2 teaspoon crushed red pepper flakes

Place potatoes in an ungreased 11-in. x 7-in. x 2-in. baking dish. Mix butter, oregano, garlic and red pepper flakes; pour over potatoes. Bake, uncovered, at 450° for 30 minutes or until potatoes are tender, stirring every 10 minutes. **Yield:** 4-6 servings.

HODGEPODGE STEW

Julia Trachsel, Victoria, British Columbia
(PICTURED ON PAGE 43)

This is a dish that I enjoyed as a child and still remember with pleasure. Mom's homemade bread made the perfect complement to this meal.

    6 cups water
    2 teaspoons salt, *divided*
    1 pound green beans, cut into 1-inch pieces
    6 carrots, cut into 1-inch pieces
    3 medium potatoes, peeled and quartered
    1 cup fresh *or* frozen corn
    2 cups fresh *or* frozen peas
    6 tablespoons butter *or* margarine
    2 cups whipping cream

    2 tablespoons minced fresh chives
    1/2 teaspoon pepper
    1/4 teaspoon paprika

In a large saucepan or Dutch oven, bring water and 1 teaspoon salt to a boil. Add beans, carrots, and potatoes; cook 15 minutes. Add corn and peas; cook an additional 3-5 minutes or until tender. Drain, reserving 2 cups liquid. Set vegetables aside. In the same saucepan, combine reserved liquid, butter, cream, chives, pepper, paprika and remaining salt. Add vegetables and heat through. **Yield:** 8-10 servings (3 quarts).

SWEET POTATO BREAD

Peggy Brett, Halifax, North Carolina
(PICTURED ON PAGE 43)

My grandmother's recipe is delicious for family gatherings. You might also want to bake some for holiday bazaars—it's a great seller!

    2 eggs
  1-1/2 cups sugar
    1/2 cup vegetable oil
    1/3 cup water
    1 teaspoon vanilla extract
  1-3/4 cups all-purpose flour
  1-1/2 teaspoons ground cinnamon
  1-1/2 teaspoons ground nutmeg
    1 teaspoon baking soda
    1/2 teaspoon salt
    1 cup cold mashed sweet potatoes
    1/2 cup raisins
    1/2 cup chopped nuts

In a mixing bowl, beat eggs, sugar, oil and water at medium speed. Add vanilla. Combine dry ingredients; stir into egg mixture just until moistened. Stir in sweet potatoes, raisins and nuts. Pour into two greased 5-1/4-in. x 3-3/4-in. coffee cans. Bake at 350° for 55-60 minutes or until breads test done. Cool 10 minutes on a wire rack. Remove from cans; cool completely. **Yield:** 2 loaves.

AU GRATIN POTATOES

Jeannine Clayton, Byron, Minnesota
(PICTURED ON PAGE 43)

A friend gave me this recipe when I needed a potato dish for a potluck. That was many years ago, but I still get compliments whenever someone tries it for the first time.

  12 medium red *or* white potatoes
    1 teaspoon salt

1/2 teaspoon pepper
1/2 teaspoon garlic salt *or* onion salt
2 cups (8 ounces) shredded cheddar cheese
1 cup whipping cream

Cook potatoes in jackets until just tender. Drain and chill several hours or overnight. Peel and coarsely shred. Combine salt, pepper and garlic or onion salt. Layer potatoes and seasonings in a greased 13-in. x 9-in. x 2-in. baking dish. Sprinkle with cheese; pour cream over all. Bake at 350° for 1 hour or until golden. **Yield:** 12-15 servings.

POTATO FRITTATA
Helen Claveloux, Newark, Delaware
(PICTURED ON PAGE 42)

In 1975, I took a trip to Spain to visit my nephew who was in the Air Force. While touring the small towns and villages, we could always buy a fresh slice of potato frittata. It was so tasty and filling, I just had to make my own version of it when I returned home!

4 medium potatoes, peeled, quartered and sliced
1 cup chopped onion
1 medium green pepper, chopped
1 to 2 tablespoons cooking oil
3/4 cup diced fully cooked ham *or* cooked bulk pork sausage
10 eggs
1 teaspoon paprika
Salt and pepper to taste
3 slices process American cheese, cut diagonally

In a 10- or 12-in. skillet, saute potatoes, onion and green pepper in oil until potatoes are tender. Add the meat and heat through. In a bowl, beat eggs, paprika, salt and pepper. Pour over potato mixture. Do not stir. Cover and cook over medium-low heat for 10-15 minutes or until eggs are nearly set. Broil 6 in. from the heat for 2 minutes or until top is lightly browned. Arrange cheese slices on top; let stand 5 minutes before serving. **Yield:** 6-8 servings.

HOLIDAY SWEET POTATOES
Mary Cass, Sun Lakes, Arizona

The sweet potatoes, apples and pecans used in this dish are all grown here in southern Arizona. In the fall, we like to visit the pecan groves and pick up the "leavings" after the pickers have gone through.

6 large sweet potatoes, cooked, peeled and sliced, *divided*
3 large apples, peeled and sliced, *divided*
3/4 cup packed brown sugar
2 teaspoons ground nutmeg
1/4 cup butter *or* margarine
1 cup apple cider
1 cup chopped pecans, toasted

Layer half of the sweet potatoes and half of the apples in a greased 13-in. x 9-in. x 2-in. baking dish. Repeat layers.

Combine brown sugar and nutmeg; sprinkle on top. Dot with butter. Pour cider over all. Cover and bake at 350° for 45-50 minutes. Sprinkle with pecans just before serving. **Yield:** 6-8 servings.

SUMMER SOUP
Carrie Sherrill, Forestville, Wisconsin

An overabundant garden led to this recipe! As the vegetable crop changes with the seasons, the soup can too—try using cauliflower, broccoli or garden-fresh peas.

2 potatoes, peeled and sliced
2 carrots, sliced
1 cup green beans, cut into 1/2-inch pieces
2 garlic cloves, minced
1 small onion, finely chopped
2 tablespoons butter *or* margarine
1/4 cup all-purpose flour
1 can (14-1/2 ounces) chicken broth
1-1/2 cups milk
1 teaspoon dried basil
1/4 teaspoon pepper
1/4 teaspoon salt

In a saucepan, cook potatoes, carrots and beans in water to cover until tender, about 10 minutes. Drain. In a soup kettle or Dutch oven, saute garlic and onion in butter until tender. Stir in flour until bubbly. Gradually add chicken broth, milk and seasonings. Cook, stirring occasionally, until thickened. Add vegetables; heat through. **Yield:** 4 servings (about 1 quart).

SWEET POTATO BALLS
Lois Hoof, Houston, Texas

My mother always served these sweet potato balls at Thanksgiving—and she always had to double the recipe!

2 cups cold mashed sweet potatoes
1 egg, lightly beaten
4 tablespoons butter *or* margarine, melted, *divided*
1 tablespoon whipping cream
1/2 teaspoon salt
1/4 teaspoon ground nutmeg
6 to 8 large marshmallows
1-1/2 cups crushed cornflakes

Mix sweet potatoes, egg, 2 tablespoons butter, cream, salt and nutmeg. Divide into six to eight portions. Pat each portion around a marshmallow. Roll in remaining butter and then in cornflakes. Place in a greased 9-in. pie plate. Bake at 400° for 15 minutes. **Yield:** 6-8 servings.

![decorative border]

GARDEN VEGETABLE SOUP
Kelly Rettiger, Emporia, Kansas

This soup is packed with energy, yet has a nice, mild flavor. The recipe makes a whole gallon, but don't worry about leftovers—like most soups, it's great reheated!

1-1/2 cups chopped onion
1 cup chopped leeks
1 garlic clove, minced
1 tablespoon cooking oil
8 cups chicken broth
8 cups cubed peeled potatoes
4 carrots, sliced
2 cups diced turnips
2 cups sliced mushrooms
6 ounces spinach, cut into thin strips
1 pound smoked Polish sausage, thinly sliced and browned
1 package (8 ounces) pasta wheels, cooked and drained
1/2 teaspoon salt
1/4 teaspoon pepper
Grated Parmesan cheese, optional

In a large soup kettle or Dutch oven, cook onion, leeks and garlic in oil until tender, about 5 minutes. Add chicken broth, potatoes, carrots, turnips and mushrooms. Cover and cook over low heat until vegetables are tender, about 30-40 minutes. Add spinach and sausage; cook for 10 minutes. Add pasta, salt and pepper; heat through. Serve with Parmesan cheese if desired. **Yield:** 16 servings (1 gallon).

![decorative border]

DELMONICO POTATOES
Mrs. Arnold Sonnenberg, Brookville, Ohio

These rich, cheesy potatoes are perfect for a large family gathering or a potluck supper.

1 cup milk
1 cup heavy cream
1-1/2 teaspoons salt
1 teaspoon dry mustard
1/4 teaspoon pepper
1/4 teaspoon ground nutmeg
1-1/2 pounds shredded sharp cheddar cheese
9 medium potatoes, cooked, peeled and shredded (about 11 cups)

In a saucepan, heat milk, cream, salt, dry mustard, pepper and nutmeg over medium heat. Add cheese; stir until melted. Place potatoes in a greased 13-in. x 9-in. x 2-in. baking dish. Pour cheese sauce over potatoes. Bake at 325° for 50-55 minutes. **Yield:** 12-16 servings.

![decorative border]

CRAB AND CORN CHOWDER
Susanna Bellany, Cremona, Alberta

I started cooking at a local restaurant when I was 16 years old. This creamy chowder was one of the soups we made.

The recipe had been passed from cook to cook—but had never been written down, until now!

1 medium onion, chopped
5 tablespoons butter *or* margarine
1/3 cup all-purpose flour
3-1/2 cups milk
4 bacon strips, cooked and crumbled
2 cans (6 ounces *each*) crabmeat, drained
2 medium potatoes, diced
1 small green pepper, chopped
1 celery rib, chopped
1 can (8-1/4 ounces) whole kernel corn, drained
1 cup light cream
1 bay leaf
1 tablespoon chopped fresh parsley
1 teaspoon salt
1/4 to 1/2 teaspoon ground nutmeg
1/4 teaspoon white pepper

In a large saucepan, saute onion in butter until tender. Add flour; cook and stir until thick and bubbly. Gradually add milk; cook and stir until thickened. Add remaining ingredients. Cover and simmer until vegetables are tender, about 35-40 minutes. Remove bay leaf before serving. **Yield:** 6 servings (1-1/2 quarts).

GOURMET POTATO SOUP WITH CROUTONS
Sherrie Pfister, Hollandale, Wisconsin

During the long Wisconsin winters, my family "lives on" homemade soups because they are economical and freeze well. And, as with most soups, this one is even better the next day.

SOUP:
3 cups diced peeled potatoes
1/2 cup diced celery
1/2 cup diced onion
1 chicken bouillon cube *or* 1 teaspoon chicken bouillon granules
1-1/2 cups water
2 cups milk
1 cup (8 ounces) sour cream
1 tablespoon all-purpose flour
1 tablespoon minced fresh chives
CROUTONS:
8 cups cubed day-old French bread (1-1/2-inch pieces)
Fat for deep-frying
1/2 cup grated Parmesan cheese
1 tablespoon minced fresh parsley
1/2 teaspoon paprika
1/2 teaspoon garlic salt
1/4 teaspoon pepper

In a large kettle or Dutch oven, cook potatoes, celery, onion and bouillon in water until vegetables are tender, about 20 minutes. Add milk. In a medium bowl, combine sour cream and flour. Blend in 1/2 cup of hot soup; return to kettle. Add chives and simmer just until thickened. Meanwhile, for croutons, deep-fry bread cubes in fat until golden brown. Drain on paper towel. In a bowl, combine remaining ingredients. Add croutons and toss to coat. Ladle soup into bowls and top with croutons. **Yield:** 6-8 servings (2 quarts).

LAMB AND POTATO STEW
JoAnn Plank, Mattawana, Pennsylvania

My family loves lamb, but I find very few recipes that use it. I picked this one up at the fair and make it quite often. Bake a pan of biscuits...and you have a complete meal!

>   2 pounds lean lamb stew meat, cut into 1-inch pieces
>   1/2 cup chopped onion
>   4 to 6 medium potatoes, peeled and diced
>   4 carrots, diced
> 1-1/4 cups water
>   1 can (16 ounces) tomatoes with liquid, cut up
>   1/2 cup diced celery
> 1-1/2 teaspoons salt
>   1/2 teaspoon pepper
>   1/2 teaspoon garlic powder
>   1/2 teaspoon dried thyme
>   1/2 teaspoon dried basil
>   1 to 2 bay leaves

In a large kettle or Dutch oven, combine all ingredients. Cover and bake at 250° for 3-4 hours or until tender. Remove bay leaves before serving. **Yield:** 8 servings (2 quarts).

POTATO STORAGE: *A cool, dark, well-ventilated place is the best storage area for fresh potatoes. When possible, refrigerate new potatoes. Never freeze uncooked potatoes.*

BAVARIAN POTATO SOUP
Janice Gagel, New Bremen, Ohio

My husband and I first enjoyed this soup on a tour of Bavaria. When I asked for the recipe, it was delivered to our table, written in English—but with no amounts for any of the ingredients! After a few trials, I got it "right" and forwarded the recipe to several of the people that were in our tour group.

>   1/2 pound bacon, diced
> 2-1/2 pounds potatoes, peeled and cut into 1/2-inch cubes
>   2 large carrots, finely chopped
>   3 celery ribs, finely chopped
>   4 leeks, finely chopped
>   2 teaspoons salt
>   1/2 teaspoon dried marjoram
>   1/4 teaspoon pepper
> **Chopped fresh parsley, optional**

In a Dutch oven or large saucepan, fry bacon; drain all but 2 tablespoons drippings. Add vegetables, seasonings and enough water to cover (about 4 cups). Simmer, covered, for

2 hours. Garnish with parsley if desired. **Yield:** 8 servings (2 quarts).

POTATO PANCAKES
Barbara Braatz, Greendale, Wisconsin

I have always been fascinated with the life-style of the Amish, especially when it comes to their cooking! I came across this old Amish recipe years ago, and it's my husband's very favorite side dish.

>   2 large potatoes, peeled and cubed (about 2 cups), *divided*
>   1 medium onion, cubed
>   2 eggs
>   3 tablespoons all-purpose flour
>   2 tablespoons minced fresh parsley
>   1/2 teaspoon baking powder
>   1/2 teaspoon salt
>   1/2 teaspoon pepper
>   1/4 teaspoon Worcestershire sauce
>   1/8 teaspoon ground nutmeg

In a blender or food processor, place 1/2 cup potatoes, onion, eggs, flour, parsley, baking powder, salt, pepper, Worcestershire sauce and nutmeg. Process until smooth. Add remaining potatoes and pulse until chopped (two to three times). Pour by 1/4 cupfuls onto a hot well-oiled skillet or griddle. Fry over medium heat until golden on both sides. **Yield:** about 8 pancakes.

POTATO VEGETABLE QUICHE
Marion DeArmond, Sicamous, British Columbia

When I can't decide what I'd like for supper, this hearty quiche is my first choice.

>   5 medium *unpeeled* potatoes (about 2 pounds), cooked and mashed
>   2 tablespoons butter *or* margarine
>   1 teaspoon salt
>   1 teaspoon dried parsley flakes
>   1/4 teaspoon pepper
>   1/4 teaspoon ground nutmeg
>   1 cup (4 ounces) shredded cheddar cheese
>   1/2 cup chopped onion
>   1/2 cup sliced fresh mushrooms
>   1/2 cup diced cooked bacon
>   1/4 cup chopped green pepper
>   1/4 cup chopped sweet red pepper
>   3 eggs, lightly beaten
>   1/2 cup cream-style corn
>   1/4 cup milk
>   1/4 teaspoon paprika

Place warm potatoes in a large bowl; add butter, salt, parsley, pepper and nutmeg. Mix well. Spread into a greased 9-in. pie plate. Combine cheese, onion, mushrooms, bacon and peppers. Spoon into crust. Combine eggs, corn and milk; pour over vegetables. Sprinkle with paprika. Bake at 375° for 45-50 minutes or until a knife inserted near the center comes out clean. Serve warm. **Yield:** 6-8 servings.

BROCCOLI/CAULIFLOWER

Why not put real snap into your meals with these crisp, versatile vegetables?
Naturally high in vitamins and minerals, bright-green broccoli florets and cream-colored
cauliflower morsels can make your meals healthful...and your table so colorful!

MARINATED VEGETABLE SALAD

Betty Olason, Hensel, North Dakota

(PICTURED AT LEFT)

The combination of ingredients in this salad gives it a unique tangy flavor. Perhaps that's why I get requests for the recipe whenever I serve this dish to company or bring it to a potluck dinner.

DRESSING:
2 cups sugar
1 cup cider vinegar
1 tablespoon salt
1 tablespoon dry mustard
1 cup vegetable oil
1 teaspoon celery seed
1/2 teaspoon Italian seasoning

VEGETABLES:
1 large head cauliflower, cut into florets
1 large bunch broccoli, cut into florets
4 carrots, thinly sliced
2 cups sliced celery
1/2 cup sliced radishes
2 green onions, thinly sliced
1/2 medium green pepper, sliced
1 can (6 ounces) pitted ripe olives, drained and sliced
1 pint cherry tomatoes, halved

In a saucepan, bring the sugar, vinegar, salt and dry mustard to a boil. Cook for 1 minute. Allow to cool. Add remaining dressing ingredients. Chill. Combine all vegetables in a large bowl; add dressing and toss. Cover and refrigerate several hours, stirring occasionally. **Yield:** 16-20 servings.

CAULIFLOWER HAM CHOWDER

Lois Buch, Clarinda, Iowa

Soup is always good for warming the tummy and the heart, and this is one of our family's favorites. With a busy household, it's a simple but nutritious meal to have on hand!

MARVELOUS MEDLEY! *Pictured at left: Marinated Vegetable Salad (recipe above).*

---

2 cups cubed peeled potatoes
2 cups fresh cauliflower florets
1 small onion, finely diced
1 cup chicken broth
3 cups milk
2-1/2 cups cubed fully cooked ham
1 teaspoon salt
1/2 teaspoon pepper
Dash ground nutmeg
1/2 to 1 cup instant potato flakes
Minced fresh parsley

In a saucepan, cook the potatoes, cauliflower and onion in chicken broth until tender. Stir in milk, ham, salt, pepper and nutmeg; heat through. Stir in potato flakes; simmer for 5-10 minutes or until soup is as thick as desired. Sprinkle with parsley. **Yield:** 6-8 servings (2 quarts).

LAMB BROCCOLI STRUDEL

Mary Bengtson-Almquist, Petersburg, Illinois

When my husband was on his second helping of this dish, I surprised him by telling him the ingredients—two foods he's not especially fond of. Now he asks for this dish often!

1 pound ground lamb *or* pork
1 medium onion, chopped
2 cups chopped fresh broccoli, blanched
1 cup (4 ounces) shredded mozzarella cheese
1/2 cup sour cream
1/4 cup dry bread crumbs
1 garlic clove, minced
1 teaspoon seasoned salt
1/2 teaspoon pepper
1 package (8 ounces) phyllo pastry sheets (13 inches x 9 inches)
1/2 cup butter *or* margarine, melted

In a skillet, brown lamb or pork and onion. Drain and cool. In a large bowl, combine the broccoli, cheese, sour cream, bread crumbs, garlic, seasoned salt and pepper. Mix in meat and onion. Place 1 sheet of phyllo dough on a piece of waxed paper. Brush with butter; continue layering with 9 more sheets of dough, brushing each with butter. Spoon half of the meat mixture on dough. Roll up, jelly-roll style, starting with the short end. Place the roll, seam side down, on a greased baking sheet. Repeat with remaining dough and filling. Brush tops of rolls with remaining butter. Bake at 350° for 45-50 minutes or until golden brown. Cool for 10 minutes before slicing. **Yield:** 6-8 servings.

BROCCOLI AND CAULIFLOWER SALAD

Linda Lanting, Mount Vernon, Washington

My family loves the "crunch" of this salad...and each crisp ingredient adds to that delight! The secret of this recipe is to make the dressing a day ahead to allow the flavors to blend.

2 cups mayonnaise
1/2 cup sugar
1/3 cup grated Parmesan cheese
2 tablespoons vinegar
2 tablespoons finely chopped onion
1/2 cup raisins
1 bunch broccoli, cut into florets
1 small head cauliflower, cut into florets
1 can (8 ounces) sliced water chestnuts, drained
1/2 pound bacon, cooked and crumbled
2/3 cup slivered toasted almonds

In a small bowl, combine mayonnaise, sugar, Parmesan cheese, vinegar, onion and raisins; refrigerate several hours or overnight. Just before serving, combine broccoli, cauliflower, water chestnuts, bacon and almonds in a large bowl. Pour dressing over and toss to coat. **Yields:** 8-10 servings.

HOT BROCCOLI DIP

Betty Reinholt, Culver, Indiana

So many friends ask about the special flavor of this dip. The mystery is rosemary! I especially like to serve this hot dip during the holidays, but my family loves it all year-round. They even like the leftovers warmed up the next day!

1/2 cup finely chopped onion
1/2 cup finely chopped celery
2 tablespoons butter *or* margarine
1 package (16 ounces) process American cheese, cut into cubes
2 cups chopped fresh broccoli, blanched
1/2 teaspoon dried rosemary, crushed
1 loaf (1 pound) round bread
Raw vegetables, optional

In a small saucepan, saute onion and celery in butter until tender. Add cheese and cook over low heat until melted. Stir in broccoli and rosemary. Cut top off bread; scoop out center. Cut center piece into cubes. Pour dip into center of bread. Serve with bread cubes and/or raw vegetables if desired. **Yield:** 10-12 appetizer servings (3 cups).

BROCCOLI BEEF CURRY

Andrea Su, Binghamton, New York

We developed our own version of this dish after tasting it at a local Indian restaurant. The curry's not overpowering—it has a wonderful flavor.

1-1/2 pounds round steak, cut into 1-inch cubes
2 to 3 garlic cloves, minced
2 teaspoons minced fresh gingerroot
1 teaspoon curry powder
1 teaspoon chili powder
1 teaspoon salt
2 large onions, diced
3 tablespoons vegetable *or* sesame oil
1 cup water
1 pound fresh broccoli, cut into florets
Cornstarch and water, optional
Hot cooked rice

Toss meat with garlic, gingerroot, curry powder, chili powder and salt. In a large skillet or wok, cook meat with onions in oil until browned. Stir in water. Cover and simmer 1-1/2 hours or until beef is tender. Add broccoli and more water if necessary; cook, covered, until broccoli is crisptender. If desired, thicken with cornstarch dissolved in water. Serve over rice. **Yield:** 6 servings.

TORTELLINI VEGETABLE SALAD

Sharon List, Westminster, California

Not only is this salad wonderfully colorful, it takes very little time to prepare. I like to serve it for luncheons or light suppers...it's sure to please pasta lovers!

1 bottle (8 ounces) prepared Italian dressing
2 tablespoons Dijon mustard
1 cup fresh broccoli florets
1 cup sliced fresh mushrooms
1 cup cherry tomato halves
1 cup sliced zucchini
1 package (9 ounces) refrigerated cheese- *or* meat-filled tortellini, cooked and drained
1/2 cup sliced pitted ripe olives

In a large bowl, combine Italian dressing and mustard. Add remaining ingredients; toss to coat. Cover and chill. **Yield:** 6-8 servings.

BROCCOLI TUNA ROLL-UPS

Jenna Lee Garrett, Norman, Oklahoma

It's easy to enjoy your guests when you have this main dish on the menu. It's one you can make ahead and then warm up as you mingle. I often take this as a "dish to pass" and it's a crowd-pleaser every time!

1 can (10-3/4 ounces) condensed cream of mushroom soup, undiluted
1 cup milk
1 can (12-1/4 ounces) tuna, drained and flaked
2-1/2 cups broccoli florets, cooked
1 cup (4 ounces) shredded cheddar cheese, *divided*
1 can (2.8 ounces) french-fried onions, *divided*
6 small flour tortillas (6 to 7 inches)
1/2 cup chopped tomatoes, optional

In a small bowl, combine soup and milk; set aside. In a medium bowl, combine tuna, broccoli, 1/2 cup cheddar cheese, half of the onions and 3/4 cup of the soup mixture; mix well. Divide mixture among tortillas and roll up. Place, seam side down, in a greased 12-in. x 8-in. x 2-in. baking dish. Pour remaining soup mixture over tortillas. Sprinkle with tomatoes if desired. Cover and bake at 350° for 35 minutes. Uncover; sprinkle with remaining cheese and onions. Return to the oven for 5 minutes. **Yield:** 3-6 servings.

CAULIFLOWER AND WILD RICE SOUP
Judy Schield, Merrill, Wisconsin

This recipe is versatile because it makes a fine complement to a main meal, or it can be a meal in itself.

- 1 medium onion, chopped
- 1 cup thinly sliced celery
- 1 cup sliced fresh mushrooms
- 1/2 cup butter *or* margarine
- 1/2 cup all-purpose flour
- 1 quart chicken broth
- 2 cups cooked wild rice
- 2 cups cauliflower florets, cooked
- 1 cup light cream

In a large saucepan, saute onion, celery and mushrooms in butter until tender. Sprinkle with flour; stir to coat well. Gradually add chicken broth. Cook and stir until thickened. Stir in wild rice, cauliflower and cream until well blended. Cook gently until heated through; do not boil. **Yield:** 6-8 servings (about 2 quarts).

CAULIFLOWER CORN SUPREME
Joanie Elbourn, Gardner, Massachusetts

My great-aunt gave me the original recipe to be used as a side dish, but I changed it to work as a vegetarian main dish. We enjoy it often with salad and bread.

- 3 tablespoons all-purpose flour
- 1 teaspoon salt
- 1/2 teaspoon garlic powder
- 1/4 teaspoon pepper
- 4 cups thinly sliced fresh cauliflower
- 1 small sweet onion, chopped
- 1-1/2 cups fresh corn
- 1 small sweet red pepper, chopped
- 1/2 cup grated Parmesan cheese
- 2 tablespoons minced fresh parsley
- 2 tablespoons butter *or* margarine
- 3/4 cup milk
- 1/4 cup white wine *or* apple juice
- 1 cup (4 ounces) shredded mozzarella *or* Swiss cheese

Combine first four ingredients; set aside. In a greased 8-in. square baking dish, layer cauliflower and onion. Sprinkle with flour mixture. Top with corn and red pepper. Sprinkle with Parmesan cheese and parsley; dot with butter. Combine milk and wine or apple juice; pour over vegetables. Sprinkle with cheese. Cover and bake at 350° for 45 minutes. Uncover; bake 15 minutes longer or until vegetables are tender. **Yield:** 6-8 servings.

BROCCOLI AND CRAB BISQUE
Dorothy Child, Malone, New York

Since our son is a broccoli grower, our friends keep supplying us with recipes using broccoli. To this family favorite, add a tossed salad, rolls, fruit and cookies, and you have an easy but delicious supper full of nutrition.

- 1 cup sliced leeks (white part only)
- 1 cup sliced fresh mushrooms
- 1 cup fresh broccoli florets
- 1 garlic clove, minced
- 1/4 cup butter *or* margarine
- 1/4 cup all-purpose flour
- 1/4 teaspoon dried thyme, crushed
- 1/8 teaspoon pepper
- 1 bay leaf
- 2 cans (10-1/2 ounces *each*) condensed chicken broth, undiluted
- 1 cup light cream
- 3/4 cup shredded Swiss cheese
- 1 package (6 ounces) frozen crabmeat, thawed, drained and flaked

In a saucepan, cook leeks, mushrooms, broccoli and garlic in butter until broccoli is crisp-tender. Remove from the heat; blend in flour and seasonings. Stir in broth and cream. Cook and stir until mixture comes to a boil and is thickened; cook 1 minute. Add cheese; stir until melted. Add crabmeat and heat through; do not boil. Remove bay leaf before serving. **Yield:** 4-5 servings (5 cups).

BROCCOLI-STUFFED POTATOES
Dia Steele, Comanche, Texas

This is one of my favorite light suppers...an easy spur-of-the-moment meal that satisfies even the heartiest appetites.

- 2 tablespoons butter *or* margarine
- 2 tablespoons all-purpose flour
- 1 cup milk
- 1/4 teaspoon dry mustard
- 1/4 teaspoon salt
- 1/4 teaspoon pepper
- 1/2 cup shredded cheddar cheese
- 3 cups chopped fresh broccoli, cooked
- 1 cup chopped fully cooked ham
- 4 to 6 baking potatoes, baked

In a small saucepan, melt butter. Add flour and stir to make a smooth paste. Stir in milk and cook over low heat until thickened. Add mustard, salt and pepper. Stir in cheese and cook until melted. Fold in broccoli and ham. Serve over hot baked potatoes. **Yield:** 4-6 servings.

GARDEN GOODNESS. *Clockwise from lower right: Broccoli Muffins, Broccoli Cheese Soup, Basil Broccoli/Tomato Platter, Broccoli Pie and Vegetable Stew (all recipes on pages 54 and 55).*

BROCCOLI MUFFINS

Theresa Rentfro, Cedar Creek, Texas

(PICTURED ON PAGE 53)

Because my family loves muffins, I'm alway on the lookout for new variations. When I tried these nutritional muffins the first time, they were really a hit and became a favorite addition to our big family meals.

  1-3/4 cups all-purpose flour
    1 cup quick-cooking oats
  1/4 cup sugar
    2 teaspoons baking powder
  1/4 teaspoon salt
    1 cup milk
  1/3 cup vegetable oil
    1 egg, lightly beaten
    1 cup chopped fresh broccoli, blanched
  1/2 cup shredded cheddar cheese

In a large bowl, combine flour, oats, sugar, baking powder and salt. In a small bowl, mix milk, oil and egg; stir into dry ingredients just until moistened. Fold in broccoli and cheese. Spoon into greased or paper-lined muffin cups. Bake at 400° for 18-20 minutes or until top springs back when lightly touched. **Yield:** 1 dozen.

BROCCOLI PIE

Elizabeth Baltes, Greenfield, Wisconsin

(PICTURED ON PAGE 52)

Everyone seems to enjoy pie for dessert. But I surprised my family the first time I brought this pie to the table as the main course! They loved it and asked for it again and again.

    1 large onion, chopped
    3 tablespoons cooking oil
    4 eggs, lightly beaten
    4 cups chopped fresh broccoli, cooked
    2 cups (8 ounces) shredded mozzarella cheese
    1 carton (15 ounces) ricotta cheese
  1/3 cup grated Parmesan cheese
  1/4 teaspoon salt
Dash ground nutmeg
    1 unbaked pie pastry (9 inches)

In a skillet, saute onion in oil until tender, about 5 minutes. Transfer to a large bowl; add eggs, broccoli, cheeses, salt and nutmeg. Pour into pie shell. Bake at 350° for 50-55 minutes or until a knife inserted near the center comes out clean. **Yield:** 6-8 servings.

BASIL BROCCOLI/ TOMATO PLATTER

Pauline Barker, Springfield, Missouri

(PICTURED ON PAGE 52)

My family especially loves this at the end of summer, during the peak of tomato season.

    5 fresh tomatoes, peeled and sliced
    1 red onion, thinly sliced into rings
    2 pounds fresh broccoli, cut into florets, cooked
DRESSING:
  1/2 cup vegetable oil
  1/2 cup red wine vinegar
    3 tablespoons fresh minced basil *or* 1 tablespoon dried basil
    1 tablespoon fresh minced parsley or 1 teaspoon dried parsley flakes
  1-1/2 teaspoons salt
Pepper to taste

In a large shallow dish or a 13-in. x 9-in. x 2-in. pan, layer tomatoes and onion along one side; place broccoli on the other side. In a small bowl, combine dressing ingredients; pour over vegetables. Cover and chill for several hours, occasionally spooning dressing over vegetables. Serve vegetables on a lettuce-lined platter if desired. **Yield:** 6-8 servings.

BROCCOLI CHEESE SOUP

Evelyn Massner, Oakville, Iowa

(PICTURED ON PAGE 52)

This simple soup has basic ingredients, but it tastes so good. The green broccoli florets and the brilliant orange carrots make this creamy soup a colorful addition to any table.

  1-1/2 cups chopped onion
  1/2 cup butter *or* margarine
  3/4 cup all-purpose flour
    1 can (10-1/2 ounces) condensed chicken broth, undiluted
    1 quart milk
    2 cups sliced carrots, parboiled
    1 cup sliced celery, parboiled
    2 cups broccoli florets, parboiled
  1/2 pound process American cheese, cut into cubes

In a large saucepan, saute onion in butter. Add flour and stir to make smooth paste. Gradually add chicken broth and milk. Cook until mixture thickens, about 8-10 minutes. Add carrots, celery and broccoli; heat through. Add cheese; heat until cheese is melted and vegetables are tender. **Yield:** 6-8 servings (2 quarts).

VEGETABLE STEW

Kenneth Wrigley, Langley, British Columbia

(PICTURED ON PAGE 53)

Everyone in my family welcomes a dinner that centers around stew. This particular stew is so colorful you can bring the pot right to the table and serve it from there!

  1-1/2 pounds lean boneless lamb *or* pork, cut into 1-inch cubes
    2 tablespoons cooking oil
    1 medium onion, chopped
    2 medium potatoes, peeled and cubed
    1 medium leek, sliced

6 cups beef broth
2 tablespoons tomato paste
1 teaspoon salt
1/2 teaspoon dried thyme
1/4 teaspoon pepper
4 cups chopped cabbage
2 to 3 cups cauliflower florets
3 carrots, sliced
1 celery rib, sliced
1 package (10 ounces) frozen green beans, thawed
Chopped fresh parsley
Cornstarch and water, optional

In a Dutch oven, brown meat in oil over medium-high. Add onion and cook until tender; drain. Add the next seven ingredients. Cover and simmer until the meat is tender, about 1 hour. Add cabbage, cauliflower, carrots, celery, beans and parsley; cover and simmer until the vegetables are tender, about 30 minutes. If desired, thicken with cornstarch dissolved in water. **Yield:** about 8-10 servings (3-1/2 quarts).

CREAMY CAULIFLOWER SOUP

Angel Berube, Prince George, British Columbia

We use this rich and filling soup as a meal in itself. Accompanied by a salad and rolls, it makes a fine luncheon. It also makes a very nice prelude for your dinner menu when you entertain.

1 medium head cauliflower, broken into florets (about 5 cups)
2/3 cup chopped onion
1/4 cup butter *or* margarine
1/4 cup all-purpose flour
2 cups chicken broth
2 cups light cream
1/2 teaspoon Worcestershire sauce
3/4 teaspoon salt
1 cup (4 ounces) shredded cheddar cheese
Minced fresh chives *or* parsley

In a saucepan, cook cauliflower in enough water to cover until tender. Drain and reserve liquid; set aside. In the same saucepan, saute onion in butter until tender. Add flour; cook and stir until bubbly. Add broth; bring to a boil over medium heat. Reduce heat and stir in 1 cup cooking liquid, cream and Worcestershire sauce. Stir in cauliflower and salt. Remove from the heat. Add cheese and stir until melted. Sprinkle with chives or parsley. **Yield:** 6-8 servings (2 quarts).

BROCCOLI-ONION DELUXE

Shirley Spade, Nashua, New Hampshire

A friend gave me this recipe years ago. It's a marvelous dish to go with any meat...also a vegetable dish that will "keep" if your dinner party happens to be running late!

1 package (16 ounces) frozen pearl onions
1 pound fresh broccoli, cut into spears

6 tablespoons butter *or* margarine, *divided*
2 tablespoons all-purpose flour
1/4 teaspoon salt
Pinch pepper
1 cup milk
1 package (3 ounces) cream cheese, softened
1/2 cup shredded cheddar cheese
1 cup soft bread crumbs

In a covered saucepan, cook onions in a small amount of water for 5 minutes. Add broccoli; cook 5 more minutes. Drain. Place in a 2-qt. baking dish. In a small saucepan, melt 4 tablespoons butter; stir in flour, salt and pepper. Gradually add milk; cook and stir until thickened. Add cream cheese; stir until melted. Pour sauce over vegetables; sprinkle with cheddar cheese. Cover and bake at 350° for 30 minutes. Melt remaining butter; combine with crumbs. Sprinkle over casserole. Return to the oven, uncovered, for 15 minutes. **Yield:** 6-8 servings.

CHICKEN AND BROCCOLI ROLL-UPS

Irene Michalski, Marinette, Wisconsin

The subtle taste of Swiss cheese and the seasonings used in this recipe blend together so well that they seem to suit most anybody's taste.

6 boneless skinless chicken breast halves, pounded thin
2 tablespoons cooking oil
6 to 12 spears fresh broccoli, blanched
6 slices Swiss cheese
SAUCE:
1 cup chopped onion
2 tablespoons butter *or* margarine
2 tablespoons all-purpose flour
1/2 cup chicken broth
1/2 cup milk
1/4 to 1/2 teaspoon dried basil
1/4 teaspoon celery salt
1/4 teaspoon white pepper

In a skillet, brown chicken breasts in oil on one side. On each unbrowned side, place 1 piece of Swiss cheese and 1 to 2 spears of broccoli. Roll up (secure with a toothpick if desired); set aside. In a saucepan, saute onion in butter until tender. Add flour and stir to make a smooth paste. Gradually add broth and milk; stir until thick. Add basil, celery salt and pepper. Place half of the sauce in the bottom of a greased 11-in. x 7-in. x 2-in. baking dish. Place chicken rolls over sauce. Cover with remaining sauce. Cover and bake at 350° for 20 minutes. Uncover and bake 10 minutes more or until chicken is no longer pink. **Yield:** 6 servings.

CABBAGE

Cooked or raw, this leafy delight "heads" the list for vegetable versatility! Cabbage is naturally high in vitamins and low in calories, plus it lends some real color to your table—the proof's in these pictures.

RED CABBAGE WITH APPLES
Virginia Jung, Milwaukee, Wisconsin
(PICTURED AT LEFT)

Our family has always loved red cabbage. Not only is it a perfect accompaniment to a favorite roast, it is so colorful on the plate. An added plus for the cook...it tastes even better the next day!

> 1 to 2-1/2 pounds red cabbage, shredded
> 3/4 cup boiling water
> 3 large cooking apples, sliced
> 3 tablespoons butter *or* margarine, melted
> 1/4 cup vinegar
> 1-1/2 teaspoons all-purpose flour
> 1/4 cup packed brown sugar
> 2 teaspoons salt
>
> **Dash pepper**

Place cabbage in a large saucepan; add boiling water. Cover and simmer for 10 minutes. Add apples; cook 10 minutes more or until tender. Add remaining ingredients and heat through. **Yield:** 6 servings.

OVERNIGHT SLAW
Nancy Brown, Janesville, Wisconsin
(PICTURED AT LEFT)

I love to make this recipe during the fall and winter months when salad ingredients are less abundant. I also enjoy the ease of preparation when using my food processor.

> 1 medium head cabbage, shredded
> 4 mild white onions, thinly sliced
> 2 large carrots, shredded
> 1/2 cup vinegar
> 1/2 cup sugar
> 1 teaspoon dry mustard
> 1 teaspoon celery seed
> 1 teaspoon salt
> 1/8 teaspoon pepper
> 1/2 cup vegetable oil

COLORFUL CABBAGE. *Pictured at left: Overnight Slaw and Red Cabbage with Apples (recipes above).*

In a large bowl, combine cabbage, onions and carrots; set aside. In a saucepan, combine vinegar, sugar, mustard, celery seed, salt and pepper; bring to a boil, stirring until sugar is dissolved. Remove from the heat and stir in oil. Pour over cabbage mixture. Cool to room temperature. Cover and refrigerate overnight; stir several times. **Yield:** 6-8 servings.

CABBAGE ZUCCHINI BORSCHT
Agatha Wiebe, Winkler, Manitoba

I know my family will get a hearty, healthy meal when I serve this soup. There are so many good vegetables to stir in!

> 1 meaty beef soup bone
> 2 quarts water
> 4 cups shredded cabbage
> 2 cups cubed peeled potatoes
> 2 cups sliced carrots
> 2 cups diced peeled tomatoes
> 1 onion, chopped
> 1/2 cup chopped fresh parsley
> 2 tablespoons dill weed
> 1 tablespoon anise seed, tied in a cheesecloth bag
> 1-1/2 teaspoons salt
> 1/2 teaspoon pepper
> 2 cups chopped cooked beets
> 3 cups shredded zucchini

Place soup bone and water in a Dutch oven or soup kettle; bring to a boil. Reduce heat and simmer, uncovered, for 40-45 minutes. Skim off fat. Add cabbage, potatoes, carrots, tomatoes, onion, parsley, dill, anise seed, salt and pepper. Simmer, uncovered, 2-1/2 to 3 hours. Remove meat from soup bone; discard bone and add meat to soup. Stir in beets and zucchini. Simmer 15-20 minutes longer or until zucchini is tender. Remove anise seed before serving. **Yield:** 12-14 servings (4 quarts).

PEASANT SOUP
Ramona Stude, Mineral Point, Wisconsin

I make this good hearty soup with chunks of beef often during fall and winter. The cabbage-sauerkraut is a nice combination and provides an interesting texture .

> 1 beef roast (1-1/2 pounds)
> 1 to 2 tablespoons cooking oil
> 1 onion, chopped
> 1 pound carrots, sliced
> 3 celery ribs, chopped
> 4 tomatoes, peeled and cut into wedges
> 1 tablespoon salt
> 1/2 teaspoon pepper
> 1 teaspoon dill seed
> 1 tablespoon chopped fresh parsley
> 2 pounds cabbage, shredded
> 1 pound sauerkraut, rinsed and drained
> 1 garlic clove, minced
> 2 tablespoons butter *or* margarine

In a large kettle, brown meat in oil on both sides. Add onion, carrots, celery, tomatoes, salt, pepper, dill seed, parsley and enough water to cover. Cook, covered, about 2 hours. In a large skillet, saute cabbage, sauerkraut and garlic in butter until cabbage is wilted. Add cabbage mixture to meat. Simmer, covered, 1-1/2 hours. Remove meat and cut into bite-size pieces; return to kettle and heat through. **Yield:** 12-14 servings (3-1/2 quarts).

GERMAN COLESLAW
Joyce Brown, Genesee, Idaho

This recipe has been handed down through generations of German families in northern Idaho. Everyone around here makes it. It's good served either warm or cold.

> 1 medium head cabbage, finely shredded
> 3 to 4 green onions, sliced
> 3/4 cup sugar
> 3/4 cup vinegar
> 1-1/2 teaspoons celery seed
> 1-1/2 teaspoons salt
> 3/4 cup vegetable oil

In a large bowl, combine cabbage and onions. In a saucepan, mix sugar, vinegar, celery seed and salt; bring to a boil. Add oil; return to boiling and cook until sugar dissolves. Pour over cabbage; toss gently. Chill. **Yield:** 14-18 servings.

CABBAGE AU GRATIN
Linda Funderburke, Brockport, New York

I think this recipe is the perfect example of "Mom's Sunday Best". It was a favorite with me and my 10 brothers and sisters. We thought Mom was the world's best cook and she always outdid herself on Sundays!

> **1 medium head cabbage, shredded (about 8 cups)**

> 1 can (10-3/4 ounces) condensed cream of celery soup, undiluted
> 2 tablespoons milk
> 1 cup shredded process American cheese
> 1 cup soft bread crumbs
> 1 tablespoon butter *or* margarine

In a large covered saucepan, cook cabbage in boiling salted water for 5 minutes; drain. Place in a greased 8-in. square baking dish. In a small saucepan, blend soup and milk; heat well. Add cheese and stir until melted. Pour over cabbage. Saute bread crumbs in butter until golden; sprinkle over cabbage. Bake at 350° for 15-20 minutes or until hot. **Yield:** 8-10 servings.

CABBAGE AND POTATO SIDE DISH
Margaret Bowers, Snohomish, Washington

This is an excellent side dish to serve with pork chops and beans. It has a wonderful old-fashioned flavor and is a refreshing change from plain potatoes and other vegetables.

> 1/2 medium onion, chopped
> 1/4 medium sweet red pepper, chopped
> 1/4 medium green pepper, chopped
> 2 garlic cloves, minced
> 2 tablespoons butter *or* margarine
> 5 to 6 cups frozen shredded hash brown potatoes
> 1/2 cup diced fully cooked ham
> 1/2 medium head cabbage, shredded (about 4 cups)
> Salt and pepper to taste

In a large nonstick skillet, saute onion, red and green pepper and garlic in butter until tender. Add hash browns; cook over high heat for 2-3 minutes. Stir in ham, cabbage, salt and pepper. Simmer for 8-10 minutes. **Yield:** 4 servings.

SPICY CABBAGE CASSEROLE
Georgia Kelly, Houma, Louisiana

This is a deliciously different main course to serve for a large crowd and so easy to prepare. Best of all, you can put it in the oven and forget about it!

> 1 small head cabbage, finely chopped
> 1 pound ground beef
> 1 can (10-3/4 ounces) condensed French onion soup, undiluted
> 1 can (16 ounces) Mexican-style tomatoes with liquid, cut up
> 1 cup uncooked long grain rice
> 1 egg, lightly beaten
> 1 large onion, chopped
> 1 medium green pepper, chopped
> 1/2 cup vegetable oil
> 1 tablespoon garlic salt
> 1 tablespoon chili powder
> 1 tablespoon salt
> Dash cayenne pepper

In a large bowl, mix all ingredients well. Pour into a small covered roasting pan. Bake at 350° for 1-1/2 hours without lifting the lid. **Yield:** 8-10 servings.

SCALLOPED CABBAGE
Barbara Calhoun, Marquette Heights, Illinois

I always read the food section in newspapers and magazines. If I find a recipe that I think my family will like, I test it out. I found this one while traveling some years ago. My family liked it and it has become one of our favorites.

- **5 to 6 cups shredded cabbage**
- **2 medium onions, finely chopped**
- **1 medium green pepper, finely chopped**
- **1/4 cup butter *or* margarine**
- **2 cups (8 ounces) shredded sharp cheddar cheese**
- **2 cups coarsely crushed sour cream and chive croutons, *divided***
- **1 cup milk *or* light cream**

In a large saucepan, cook cabbage in boiling salted water for 4-5 minutes or until almost tender; drain. In a smaller saucepan, saute onions and green pepper in butter until tender. Combine cabbage, onion-pepper mixture, cheese and 1-1/2 cups of croutons. Spoon into a 13-in. x 9-in. x 2-in. baking dish. Pour milk or cream over all; do not stir. Sprinkle with remaining croutons. Bake, uncovered, at 350° for 20-25 minutes or until bubbly. **Yield:** 6-8 servings.

CABBAGE *has been enjoyed for at least 4,000 years, as people in Europe, North Africa and China partook of this leafy vegetable. Roman statesman Marcus Porcius Cato wrote five pages on the wonders of cabbage. American colonists probably planted cabbage, and America's first written record of it appeared in 1669.*

NUTTY COLESLAW
Eleanore Hill, Fresno, California

My mom used to make this coleslaw often when I was little. I think my three siblings and I must've requested it often, because each of us was allowed to eat six peanuts as a special treat while Mom was making it. I remember we'd all line up at the kitchen table to wait for her to count them out!

- **6 cups shredded cabbage**
- **1 cup dry roasted salted peanuts**

DRESSING:
- **2 eggs**
- **1/2 cup light cream**
- **2 tablespoons all-purpose flour**
- **2 tablespoons sugar**
- **1/2 teaspoon dry mustard**

- **1/2 teaspoon paprika**
- **1/2 teaspoon salt**
- **1/3 cup cider vinegar**
- **2 tablespoons vegetable oil**
- **2 tablespoons water**

Place cabbage and peanuts in a large salad bowl; set aside. In a mixing bowl, beat eggs and cream until frothy; set aside. In a small saucepan, bring remaining dressing ingredients to a boil over medium heat, stirring constantly. Gradually beat into egg mixture. Return to heat; cook and stir over low heat until mixture thickens and coats a spoon. Set aside to cool. Pour over cabbage; toss to coat. Refrigerate. **Yield:** 8-10 servings.

SWEET-AND-SOUR CABBAGE
Eva Bailey, Olive Hill, Kentucky

After I came up with this recipe, I finally succeeded in getting my kids to eat cooked cabbage. I think the touch of sweet flavor was appealing.

- **4 bacon strips, diced**
- **5 cups shredded cabbage**
- **1 medium onion, chopped**
- **1/2 cup water**
- **1/3 cup vinegar**
- **2 tablespoons all-purpose flour**
- **2 tablespoons brown sugar**
- **1/2 teaspoon salt**
- **1/8 teaspoon pepper**

In a large skillet, cook bacon until crisp. Remove bacon; set aside. Saute cabbage and onion in drippings until tender. Add remaining ingredients; stir until thickened. Stir in bacon. Serve warm. **Yield:** 6 servings.

TUNA CRUNCH CASSEROLE
Alberta McKay, Bartlesville, Oklahoma

This is a great everyday meal...it's exceptionally easy and economical to prepare. With tuna in your pantry, you can decide to make this casserole at the last minute without a trip to the store.

- **1/4 cup sliced almonds**
- **1 small onion, chopped**
- **1 celery rib, chopped**
- **2 tablespoons butter *or* margarine**
- **2 cups shredded cabbage**
- **1 can (6-1/8 ounces) tuna, drained**
- **1 can (10-3/4 ounces) condensed cream of mushroom soup, undiluted**
- **1 can (3 ounces) chow mein noodles, *divided***

In a skillet, saute the almonds, onion and celery in butter. Meanwhile, combine cabbage, tuna, soup and half of the chow mein noodles in a bowl. Stir in almond mixture. Spoon into an ungreased 11-in. x 7-in. x 2-in. baking dish. Sprinkle remaining noodles on top. Bake at 350° for 20 minutes or until bubbly. **Yield:** 6 servings.

NEW ENGLAND BOILED DINNER

Eleene McCann, Sullivan, New Hampshire

(PICTURED ON PAGE 61)

I enjoy fixing this dish on chilly days. I also use this recipe on St. Patrick's Day since all the ingredients are appropriate for that traditional meal.

> **1 corned beef brisket (3 to 4 pounds)**
> **1/2 pound sliced bacon**
> **6 carrots**
> **1 to 2 turnips, quartered**
> **6 potatoes, peeled and halved**
> **2 medium onions, quartered**
> **1 small head cabbage, cored and quartered**

Place brisket and enclosed seasoning packet in a Dutch oven with enough water to cover. Simmer, covered, about 1 hour. Add bacon; simmer 1 to 1-1/2 hours longer or until beef is tender. Remove brisket from Dutch oven and keep warm. Discard bacon; strain stock. Return stock to Dutch oven. Add carrots and turnips; simmer for 10 minutes. Add potatoes and onions; simmer for 15 minutes more. Add cabbage; simmer for 10-15 minutes or until tender. Return brisket to stock; heat through. Place meat on a large platter with vegetables around it. **Yield:** 8-10 servings.

RUSSIAN-STYLE VEGETABLE SOUP

Elaine Dohms, Fenwood, Saskatchewan

(PICTURED ON PAGE 61)

I've always loved to experiment with food and recipes, and the following recipe is no exception. We all enjoy this soup on a cool day because it seems to warm you right up!

> **1 to 1-1/2 pounds beef stew meat, cut into bite-size pieces**
> **1-1/2 teaspoons salt**
> **3/4 teaspoon pepper**
> **7 cups water**
> **1 medium onion, chopped**
> **1 tablespoon butter *or* margarine**
> **8 cups shredded cabbage**
> **4 cups sliced carrots**
> **2 celery ribs, sliced**
> **2 medium potatoes, peeled and cubed**
> **2 cups chopped tomatoes**
> **1 cup chopped fresh beets**
> **1/4 cup minced fresh parsley**
> **1-1/2 tablespoons vinegar**
> **2 tablespoons all-purpose flour**
> **3/4 cup light cream**

In a large kettle, combine stew meat, salt, pepper and water; bring to a boil. Reduce heat; cover and simmer for 1 hour. In a small saucepan, saute onion in butter until tender; add to kettle. Add cabbage, carrots, celery, potatoes, tomatoes, beets, parsley and vinegar; bring to a boil. Reduce heat; simmer for 50-60 minutes or until vegetables are ten-

der. In a small bowl, mix flour and cream. Stir into soup; heat through. **Yield:** 6-8 servings (4 quarts).

PICKLED CABBAGE

Marion Glasgow, Lavallette, New Jersey

(PICTURED ON PAGE 61)

My mother picked up this recipe in Pennsylvania, and as long as I can remember, there was always a "bucket" of slaw in the refrigerator. Now I have an old stoneware butter crock in my refrigerator filled with the same!

> **2-1/2 cups shredded cabbage**
> **1/2 medium green pepper, diced**
> **1 celery rib, diced**
> **3/4 cup sugar**
> **1/2 cup vinegar**
> **1/2 teaspoon celery seed**
> **1/2 teaspoon salt**
> **1/8 teaspoon pepper**

In a large bowl, combine all ingredients. Toss to coat. Cover and refrigerate at least 1 hour before serving. **Yield:** 4 servings.

BEEF CABBAGE STEW

Lesa Swartwood, Fulton, Missouri

(PICTURED ON PAGE 60)

This is one of my favorite meals since I don't have to stand over the stove or dirty a lot of pots and pans to prepare it. With six in the family, we have enough dishes to wash after each meal!

> **1-1/2 pounds beef stew meat, cut into 1-inch pieces**
> **2 beef bouillon cubes**
> **1 cup hot water**
> **1 large onion, chopped**
> **1/4 teaspoon pepper**
> **1 bay leaf**
> **2 medium potatoes, peeled and cubed**
> **2 celery ribs, sliced**
> **4 cups shredded cabbage**
> **1 carrot, sliced**
> **1 can (8 ounces) tomato sauce**
> **Salt to taste**

In a large saucepan or Dutch oven, brown stew meat; drain Meanwhile, dissolve bouillon cubes in water; add to beef. Add onion, pepper and bay leaf. Cover; simmer 1-1/4 hours or until tender. Add potatoes, celery, cabbage and carrot. Cover and simmer 30 minutes or until vegetables are tender. Stir in tomato sauce and salt. Simmer, uncovered, 15-20 minutes more. Remove bay leaf before serving. **Yield:** 6-8 servings.

STUFFED CABBAGE ROLLS

Shirley Felts, Jackson, Mississippi
(PICTURED ON PAGE 60)

We have been making this dish in my family since I was a little girl. Mother served it with corn bread fritters—I like to serve it with corn bread muffins.

> **1 medium head cabbage**
> **1 to 1-1/4 pounds ground beef**
> **1 cup cooked rice**
> **1 small onion, chopped**
> **1 egg, lightly beaten**
> **2 teaspoons salt-free seasoning**
> **1/2 teaspoon pepper**
> **1/2 teaspoon dried thyme**
> **1 can (16 ounces) tomato sauce**
> **4 teaspoons brown sugar**
> **1/4 cup water**
> **1 tablespoon lemon juice *or* vinegar**

Remove core from cabbage. Steam 12 large outer leaves until limp. Drain well. In a bowl, combine ground beef, rice, onion, egg and seasonings; mix well. Put about 1/3 cup meat mixture on each cabbage leaf. Fold in sides, starting at an unfolded edge, and roll up leaf completely to enclose filling. Repeat with remaining leaves and filling. Place rolls in a large skillet or Dutch oven. Combine tomato sauce, brown sugar, water and lemon juice or vinegar; pour over cabbage rolls. Cover and simmer for 1 hour, spooning sauce over rolls occasionally during cooking. **Yield:** 4-6 servings.

CREAMY CABBAGE

Alice Lewis, Los Osos, California

This recipe, which was handed down to me from my grandmother, makes a good side dish for any meal. It's a simple way to spruce up a cabbage dish and has always been happily received at potluck suppers.

> **4 cups shredded cabbage**
> **1/2 cup diced bacon**
> **1 tablespoon all-purpose flour**
> **1/2 teaspoon salt**
> **1/4 teaspoon paprika**
> **1/8 teaspoon pepper**
> **1 cup milk**
> **1 cup soft bread crumbs**

In a large saucepan, cook cabbage for 7 minutes in boiling water; drain. In a skillet, cook bacon. Remove bacon and all but 1 tablespoon drippings. Add flour, salt, paprika and pepper to drippings. Gradually add milk; simmer and stir until thickened. Place cabbage in a 1-qt. casserole. Top with sauce. Sprinkle bread crumbs and bacon over the top. Bake at 400° for 15 minutes. **Yield:** 4 servings.

CREAMED CABBAGE SOUP

Laurie Harms, Grinnell, Iowa

Here's a delicious use of the ham and cabbage combination. A thick and hearty soup combined with subtle flavors, it is a favorite meal on our table during the winter months.

> **2 cups chicken broth**
> **1 medium onion, diced**
> **1 cup diced celery**
> **1 medium head cabbage, shredded**
> **1 carrot, diced**
> **1/4 cup butter *or* margarine**
> **3 tablespoons all-purpose flour**
> **1 cup milk**
> **2 cups light cream**
> **2 cups diced fully cooked ham**
> **1-1/2 teaspoons salt**
> **1/4 teaspoon pepper**
> **1/2 teaspoon dried thyme**
> **Chopped fresh parsley**

In a large kettle, combine broth and vegetables. Cover and simmer until vegetables are tender, about 20 minutes. In a saucepan, melt butter; stir in flour. Gradually add milk and cream; cook and stir until thickened. Stir into vegetable mixture. Add ham, salt, pepper and thyme; heat through. Garnish with parsley. **Yield:** 6-8 servings (2 quarts).

FOR CRISPIER COLE-SLAW *or other cabbage salad, cut cabbage heads instead of grating them. Cut cabbage paper-thin with a slicing knife or mechanical shredder. The resulting pieces have more form and the cabbage stays crunchier.*

SKILLET CABBAGE

Charmaine Fricke, St. Charles, Illinois

I use this dish often when the schedule gets tight and I need a "hurry up" vegetable to cook. It adds plenty of substance to a simple meal.

> **2 tablespoons butter *or* margarine**
> **4 cups shredded cabbage**
> **1 green pepper, cut into thin strips**
> **2 tablespoons water**
> **1/2 teaspoon salt**
> **1/4 teaspoon pepper**
> **1 package (3 ounces) cream cheese, cubed and softened**

Melt butter in a large skillet; add cabbage and green pepper and toss to coat. Stir in water, salt and pepper. Cover; simmer for 8-10 minutes or until cabbage is tender. Add cream cheese; stir until melted. **Yield:** 4-6 servings.

ASPARAGUS

Tender shoots of asparagus bring a little taste of spring to any table. Why not let these splendid spears delight your family in a multitude of ways? You will with these recipes!

ASPARAGUS CRESS SOUP
Teresa Lillycrop, Puslinch, Ontario
(PICTURED AT LEFT)

Here's a refreshing soup that combines two spring treats— asparagus and watercress. Serve it as the first course to a special meal with family or friends.

3/4 cup chopped green onions
1/4 cup butter *or* margarine
3 tablespoons all-purpose flour
2-1/2 cups chicken broth
1-1/2 pounds fresh asparagus, cut into 1-inch pieces
1/2 bunch watercress, stems removed (about 1 cup, lightly packed)
1-1/2 cups light cream
3/4 teaspoon salt
1/4 teaspoon white pepper
1/8 teaspoon cayenne pepper
Sour cream

In a large saucepan, saute onions in butter 3-4 minutes or until soft. Stir in flour to form a smooth paste. Cook for 2 minutes. Gradually stir in broth and bring to a boil. Add asparagus and watercress; cover and simmer 5-7 minutes or until vegetables are tender. Cool. Puree soup in a blender or food processor until smooth. Return to saucepan; stir in light cream. Heat over low to serving temperature (do not boil). Season with salt, white pepper and cayenne. Garnish each serving with a dollop of sour cream. **Yield:** 6 servings.

ASPARAGUS-TOMATO SALAD
Anne Frederick, New Hartford, New York
(PICTURED AT LEFT)

This is a delicious way to start off any meal—and a nice change of pace from the usual tossed salad.

DRESSING:
2 tablespoons lemon juice
1 tablespoon olive oil

1 teaspoon red wine vinegar
1/2 garlic clove, minced
1/2 teaspoon Dijon mustard
1/4 teaspoon dried basil
1/4 teaspoon salt
1/8 teaspoon pepper
SALAD:
12 fresh asparagus spears, cut into 1-1/2-inch pieces
3 small tomatoes, seeded and diced
1 small red onion, sliced

In a medium bowl, whisk together dressing ingredients; set aside. Place asparagus in a large saucepan with enough water to cover; cook until crisp-tender. Drain and cool. Combine asparagus, tomatoes and onion in a bowl. Pour dressing over salad; toss to coat. Serve immediately or refrigerate. **Yield:** 4 servings.

STORING FRESH ASPARAGUS:
You may refrigerate unwashed stalks in a covered container or plastic bag for up to 4 days. If stalks are limp, cut a thin slice off bottom ends and stand in cold water for a short time before refrigerating.

ASPARAGUS PASTA SALAD
Jan Nelson, Tallulah, Louisiana
(PICTURED AT LEFT)

I got this recipe from my sister-in-law while visiting her in Texas. I usually prepare this salad in the summer as a light evening meal for my family or as an extra-special lunch for friends.

1 pound fresh asparagus, cut into 1-1/2-inch pieces
1 package (16 ounces) multicolored corkscrew pasta, cooked and drained
1 cup diced cooked chicken
1 cup diced fully cooked ham
2 medium tomatoes, seeded and diced
1/2 cup sliced ripe olives
1-1/2 cups bottled zesty Italian dressing
1-1/2 teaspoons dill weed

Place asparagus in a large saucepan with enough water to cover; cook until crisp-tender. Drain and cool. In a large bowl, combine asparagus and remaining ingredients; toss to coat. Cover and refrigerate 3-4 hours or overnight. **Yield:** 12 servings.

APPETIZING ASPARAGUS. *Pictured at left, clockwise from bottom: Asparagus Cress Soup, Asparagus-Tomato Salad and Asparagus Pasta Salad (all recipes on this page).*

ASPARAGUS CONFETTI SALAD

Sally Hope James, Lockport, New York

I live near Lake Ontario, where we are surrounded by many farms that raise asparagus. In the spring, roadside stands are filled with bundles of fresh asparagus spears, kept crisp in pans of cool water. This salad has always been a favorite to serve at luncheons with friends.

DRESSING:
- 1/2 cup vegetable oil
- 2 tablespoons tarragon vinegar
- 2 tablespoons lemon juice
- 1/2 cup finely chopped cooked beets (about 2 small beets)
- 1 tablespoon snipped fresh parsley
- 1 teaspoon paprika
- 1 teaspoon sugar
- 1 teaspoon salt
- 1/2 teaspoon dry mustard
- 4 to 5 drops hot pepper sauce

SALAD:
- 1 pound fresh asparagus, cut into 1-1/2-inch pieces
- 4 cups torn lettuce
- 1 cup sliced celery
- 1/4 cup sliced green onions with tops
- 1 small red onion, sliced into rings
- 1 hard-cooked egg, chopped

Combine dressing ingredients in a glass jar; shake well to blend. Refrigerate. Place asparagus in a large saucepan with enough water to cover; cook until crisp-tender. Drain and chill immediately. Just before serving, combine asparagus, lettuce, celery, green onions and red onion. Toss to mix. Pour dressing over salad and toss lightly. Sprinkle with chopped egg. **Yield:** 4 servings.

ASPARAGUS AND WILD RICE CASSEROLE

Theresa Charlson, Forest City, Iowa

I learned the fun of cooking as a child. I love to create as I cook—this recipe is a combination of several different asparagus dishes. It's also tasty with pieces of cooked duck added to the wild rice.

- 2 tablespoons chopped onion
- 1 tablespoon butter *or* margarine
- 1 tablespoon all-purpose flour
- 1/8 teaspoon salt
- 1 cup milk
- 1/2 cup sour cream
- 2 cups cooked wild rice
- 2 pounds fresh asparagus, cut into 2-inch pieces and cooked
- 3/4 cup shredded cheddar cheese
- 6 bacon strips, diced and cooked

In a small saucepan, saute onion in butter until tender. Add flour and salt; stir to make a paste. Add milk; cook over medium heat, stirring constantly, until mixture thickens.

Cook 1 minute more. Remove from heat; stir in sour cream until smooth. In a greased 11-in. x 7-in. x 2-in. baking dish, layer wild rice, asparagus, sour cream mixture, cheese and bacon. Bake at 350° for 30 minutes. **Yield:** 6 servings.

TOMATO-ASPARAGUS SOUFFLE

Ella Schafer, Wessington Springs, South Dakota

I came across this recipe in 1978 and have been serving it ever since. The vegetable juice adds a pleasing flavor and colorful accent.

- 1 pound fresh asparagus, cut into 1/2-inch pieces
- 2 tablespoons butter *or* margarine
- 2 tablespoons all-purpose flour
- 3/4 cup vegetable juice
- 1 cup (4 ounces) shredded sharp cheddar cheese
- 1/2 teaspoon salt
- Dash cayenne pepper
- 4 eggs, *separated*
- 2 cups soft bread crumbs (about 3 slices)

Place asparagus in a large saucepan with enough water to cover; cook until crisp-tender. Drain well; set aside. In a 2-qt. saucepan, melt butter over low heat. Blend in flour to form a smooth paste. Add vegetable juice all at once. Cook and stir until mixture is thickened and bubbly. Add cheese, salt and cayenne, stirring until cheese is melted. Remove from heat. Beat egg yolks in a medium bowl; gradually stir in half of the hot cheese mixture. Return all to the saucepan. Stir in bread crumbs. Beat reserved egg whites until stiff peaks form. Fold into cheese mixture. Fold in asparagus. Pour into an ungreased 1-1/2-qt. casserole. Bake, uncovered, at 325° for 40-45 minutes or until knife inserted halfway between center and edge comes out clean. **Yield:** 6 servings.

CHUNKY ASPARAGUS SOUP

Vivian Heffner, Windsor, Pennsylvania

This recipe was handed down from my great-grandmother. I've modified it a little, but it remains a treasure from the past. My family never tires of it at asparagus time.

- 2 pounds fresh asparagus, chopped
- 1 small onion, chopped
- 1 garlic clove, minced
- 2 tablespoons butter *or* margarine
- 1/2 to 1 teaspoon curry powder
- 1 jar (4 ounces) sliced mushrooms, drained
- 1 tablespoon diced pimientos
- 1 quart chicken broth
- 1 can (12 ounces) evaporated milk
- 1/2 pound process American cheese, cut into 1-inch cubes

In a large saucepan, saute asparagus, onion and garlic in butter for 8-10 minutes or until tender. Add curry powder; simmer 5 more minutes. Add mushrooms and pimientos. Stir in chicken broth and milk. Heat, but do not boil. Add cheese cubes and stir until melted. **Yield:** 8-10 servings (2-1/2 quarts).

ASPARAGUS SALMON PIE

Shirley Martin, Fresno, California

I received this recipe from a dear neighbor years ago when we lived in the mountains near Yosemite National Park. We had four small children, and the whole family really loved this recipe. Now I make it for my husband, for guests, and for my children and grandchildren when they visit.

- 1 pound fresh asparagus
- 1/2 cup chopped onion
- 2 tablespoons butter *or* margarine
- 3 eggs, lightly beaten
- 1/2 cup milk
- 2 tablespoons minced fresh parsley
- 1/2 teaspoon dried basil
- 1/2 teaspoon salt
- 1 can (14-3/4 ounces) pink salmon, drained, boned and flaked
- 1 unbaked pastry shell (9 inches)

Place asparagus in a large saucepan with enough water to cover; cook until crisp-tender. Drain well. Reserve six spears for garnish; cut remaining spears into bite-size pieces. Set aside. In a small saucepan, saute onion in butter until tender. Set aside. In a small bowl, mix eggs, milk, parsley, basil, salt and salmon. Add sauteed onion. Place cut asparagus in pastry shell; top with salmon mixture. Arrange reserved asparagus spears, spoke fashion, on top. Cover edges of crust with foil to prevent over-browning. Bake at 425° for 30-35 minutes or until filling is set. **Yield:** 6 servings.

BEEF AND ASPARAGUS SKILLET DINNER

Barbara Calhoun, Marquette Heights, Illinois

I retired after teaching for 20 years. I have always loved cooking, and now I have more time to prepare special dishes for my husband and four grandsons, and also for church suppers. This recipe is my own invention.

- 1/2 cup soy sauce
- 1/2 cup white wine vinegar *or* dry white wine
- 3 tablespoons sugar
- 1 teaspoon garlic powder
- 1/2 teaspoon ground ginger
- 2-1/2 pounds sirloin steak, cut into thin strips
- 2 tablespoons cooking oil
- 1-1/2 pounds fresh asparagus, cut into 2-inch pieces
- 1 medium onion, cut into thin strips
- 1 green pepper, cut into thin strips
- 1/2 pound mushrooms, sliced
- 1 can (14-1/2 ounces) beef broth
- 2 tablespoons cornstarch
- Cooked rice

In a bowl, combine the first five ingredients. Add meat; cover and refrigerate for 2 hours or overnight. Drain and reserve marinade. In a large skillet or wok, brown meat in oil. Add marinade. Cover and simmer 5-10 minutes or until meat is tender. Add asparagus; cook 2 minutes. Add onion, green pepper and mushrooms. Mix beef broth and corn-

starch; add to skillet. Bring to a boil to thicken sauce. Cook 3-5 minutes longer or until vegetables are tender. Serve over rice. **Yield:** 6-8 servings.

ASPARAGUS AND HAM CASSEROLE

Helen Ostronic, Omaha, Nebraska

I created this casserole one day while trying to find a good recipe for leftover ham. Instead of resorting to scalloped potatoes and ham, or ham and noodles, I tried asparagus. Everyone liked it so well, I've made it ever since.

- 1 pound fresh asparagus, cut into 1-inch pieces
- 2 cups cubed fully cooked ham
- 3 cups cooked rice
- 1 cup diced celery
- 1-1/2 teaspoons lemon pepper
- 1 can (10-3/4 ounces) condensed cream of chicken soup, undiluted
- 1 cup chicken broth
- 1 cup (4 ounces) shredded cheddar cheese
- 1 tablespoon butter *or* margarine
- 1/2 cup bread crumbs

Place asparagus in a large saucepan with enough water to cover; cook until crisp-tender. Drain well. In a greased 2-1/2-qt. casserole, mix asparagus, ham, rice, celery and lemon pepper. In a saucepan, mix soup and broth. Add cheese and cook until melted. Pour into casserole. Melt butter in a small saucepan; add crumbs and cook and stir until browned. Sprinkle on top of casserole. Bake at 350° for 35 minutes. **Yield:** 6-8 servings.

ASPARAGUS TOMATO BAKE

Jane Vanchena, Kenosha, Wisconsin

Country roads and railroad tracks near my home are favorite places to hunt for wild asparagus—one of the true treats of spring. Both of my sons can eye wild asparagus from afar!

- 1/4 cup butter *or* margarine, melted
- 1 pound fresh asparagus, cut into 2-inch pieces
- 3 tablespoons minced onion
- 1 garlic clove, minced
- 3 tablespoons minced celery
- 2 tablespoons grated Parmesan cheese
- 2 tablespoons Italian-style dry bread crumbs
- 1 can (14-1/2 ounces) stewed tomatoes, drained and diced
- 1/2 teaspoon dried oregano
- 1/2 teaspoon salt
- 1/4 teaspoon pepper
- 1/4 teaspoon dried thyme

Pour butter into an 8-in. square baking dish. Lay asparagus over butter. Sprinkle evenly with onion, garlic, celery, cheese and bread crumbs. Cover with tomatoes. Sprinkle with oregano, salt, pepper and thyme. Cover with foil. Bake at 375° for 35-40 minutes or until the asparagus is tender. **Yield:** 6 servings.

ASPARAGUS CRAB QUICHE

Karen Templeton, Montrose, Pennsylvania
(PICTURED AT LEFT)

I almost always serve this quiche when I have company for lunch because it makes such a pretty presentation, but it's not hard to make. It gets rave reviews from family and friends—almost everyone who tastes it asks for the recipe.

3/4 pound fresh asparagus, cut into 2-inch pieces
1 unbaked pastry shell (9 inches)
1 can (6 ounces) crabmeat, drained and flaked
1 cup (4 ounces) shredded Swiss cheese
1 tablespoon all-purpose flour
3 eggs, beaten
1-1/2 cups light cream
1/2 teaspoon salt
3 drops hot pepper sauce
2 tablespoons grated Parmesan cheese
8 fresh asparagus spears for garnish

Place asparagus pieces in a large saucepan with enough water to cover; cook until crisp-tender. Drain well. Arrange cooked asparagus over bottom of pastry. Top with crabmeat. Combine Swiss cheese and flour; sprinkle over crab. In a small bowl, combine eggs, cream, salt and hot pepper sauce; mix well. Pour into pastry. Sprinkle with Parmesan cheese. Arrange asparagus spears, spoke fashion, on top of quiche. Bake at 350° for 35-40 minutes. **Yield:** 6 servings.

CHICKEN/ASPARAGUS PASTA SUPPER

Ginny Truwe, Mankato, Minnesota
(PICTURED AT LEFT)

I've used this recipe for years as a side dish for family gatherings and potluck suppers. At home, though, we make an entire meal of it...my family can't seem to get enough!

4 tablespoons cooking oil, *divided*
1-1/2 pounds fresh asparagus, cut into 2-inch pieces
8 ounces sliced fresh mushrooms
1-1/2 cups broccoli florets
2 carrots, cut into julienne strips
2 medium zucchini, sliced
3 green onions, sliced into 1/2-inch pieces
1/2 teaspoon salt
4 boneless skinless chicken breasts, cut into 1-inch pieces
1/2 cup frozen peas
SAUCE:
2 tablespoons butter *or* margarine
2 tablespoons all-purpose flour
1 chicken bouillon cube

SPEARS OF SPRING. *Pictured at left, clockwise from upper right: Asparagus Crab Quiche, Chicken/Asparagus Pasta Supper, Asparagus with Dill Butter and Asparagus Appetizer Roll-Ups (all recipes on this page).*

2 cups milk
1/4 teaspoon pepper
1 pound thin spaghetti, cooked and drained

Heat 2 tablespoons oil in a large skillet over high. Add asparagus, mushrooms, broccoli, carrots, zucchini, onions and salt. Cook and stir 5 minutes. Remove vegetables from the skillet; set aside. Add remaining oil to the skillet. Cook chicken, stirring constantly, 5-6 minutes or until it is no longer pink. Return vegetables to the skillet; add peas and cook 3-5 minutes. Set aside. For sauce, melt butter in a medium saucepan over low heat. Stir in flour to form a smooth paste. Add bouillon cube. Gradually add milk, stirring constantly until sauce is thickened. Season with pepper. Pour over chicken/vegetable mixture; toss to coat. Serve over spaghetti. **Yield:** 8 servings.

ASPARAGUS WITH DILL BUTTER

Mildred Sherrer, Bay City, Texas
(PICTURED AT LEFT)

This is simple, yet elegant enough to serve at a dinner party. The lemon juice gives it a tangy zip.

1/2 cup butter *or* margarine, softened
1/4 cup snipped fresh dill
1-1/2 teaspoons lemon juice
Cooked fresh asparagus spears

In a small bowl, combine butter, dill and lemon juice; mix until well blended. Form into a log. (If necessary, refrigerate until mixture is firm enough to shape easily.) Wrap log in plastic wrap; freeze until firm. When ready to serve, slice butter 1/4 in. thick and top hot asparagus. **Yield:** Recipe will season about 4 pounds of asparagus.

ASPARAGUS APPETIZER ROLL-UPS

Mrs. Howard Lansinger, Pineola, North Carolina
(PICTURED AT LEFT)

This is a wonderful warm appetizer for springtime entertaining. It's perfect for showers and also makes a tasty first course for Easter dinner.

12 slices white bread, crusts removed
1 container (8 ounces) soft cream cheese
2 tablespoons chopped green onions
8 bacon strips, cooked and crumbled
24 fresh asparagus spears
1/4 cup butter *or* margarine, melted
3 tablespoons grated Parmesan cheese

Flatten bread with a rolling pin. In a small bowl, combine cream cheese, onions and bacon. Spread mixture over bread slices. Cut asparagus to fit bread; place two spears on each bread slice. Roll up bread and place, seam side down, on a greased baking sheet. Brush with butter, then sprinkle with Parmesan cheese. Bake at 400° for 10-12 minutes or until lightly browned. Serve immediately. **Yield:** 1 dozen.

APPLES

If anything can match the crisp delight of a chilled tart apple, it's more of them—especially when you use them in these delicious recipes!

APPLE-STRAWBERRY SPINACH SALAD
Carolyn Popwell, Lacey, Washington
(PICTURED AT LEFT)

I created this salad myself and love to serve it in spring when strawberries are at their peak.

  1 pound fresh spinach, torn
  2 cups chopped unpeeled Granny Smith apples
  3/4 cup fresh bean sprouts
  1/2 cup sliced fresh strawberries
  1/4 cup crumbled cooked bacon
DRESSING:
  3/4 cup vegetable oil
  1/3 cup white wine vinegar
  1 small onion, grated
  1/2 cup sugar
  2 teaspoons Worcestershire sauce
  2 teaspoons salt

In a large salad bowl, combine the first five ingredients. In a small bowl, whisk together all dressing ingredients. Just before serving, pour over salad and toss. **Yield:** 4-6 servings.

SLICED APPLE FRITTERS
Dolores Tolson, Oklahoma City, Oklahoma

Apple lovers will love these! They're good for breakfast or any meal.

  1 cup (8 ounces) sour cream
  1/2 cup milk
  1 egg, lightly beaten
  2 teaspoons sugar
  1 teaspoon ground cinnamon
  1 cup self-rising flour
  1/4 cup cooking oil
  3 baking apples, peeled and thinly sliced (1/8-inch slices)
Confectioners' sugar

In a bowl, mix the first six ingredients. In a large skillet, heat oil over medium-high. Dip apples slices into batter and

SALAD DAYS. *Pictured at left: Apple-Strawberry Spinach Salad (recipe above).*

fry until golden brown, 3-4 minutes on each side. Drain on paper towels. Dust with confectioners' sugar. Serve hot. **Yield:** 4-6 servings.

OVEN-FRIED APPLES
Alice Clark, Quincy, Florida

I host a breakfast for ladies of my church during the holidays, and I often make this recipe to serve as a side dish. It's also good for topping waffles or ice cream.

  10 medium Granny Smith apples (4-1/2 pounds)
  1/2 cup plus 2 tablespoons sugar
  1/2 cup plus 2 tablespoons packed brown sugar
  2 teaspoons ground cinnamon
  1 teaspoon ground nutmeg
  1/2 cup butter *or* margarine, softened

Peel apples and cut in 1/4-in. to 1/2-in. slices. In a small bowl, combine sugars, cinnamon and nutmeg. In a greased 13-in. x 9-in. x 2-in. baking dish, alternate layers of apples and sugar mixture. Dot with butter. Cover and bake at 350° for 55 minutes. **Yield:** 6 cups.

COCONUT APPLE CAKE
Ruth Evelyn Schoeff, Huntington, Indiana

I like to share this cake with friends and neighbors. Serve it plain, frost it or top with whipped cream.

  3 cups all-purpose flour
  1 teaspoon baking soda
  1/2 teaspoon salt
  1/2 teaspoon ground cinnamon
  3 eggs
  2 cups sugar
1-1/4 cups vegetable oil
  1 teaspoon vanilla extract
  1/4 cup orange juice
  2 cups chopped peeled baking apples
  1 cup chopped walnuts
  1 cup flaked coconut

Combine flour, baking soda, salt and cinnamon. In a mixing bowl, beat eggs and sugar; add oil, vanilla and orange juice. Gradually stir in flour mixture. Stir in apples, nuts and coconut. Turn into a greased 13-in. x 9-in. x 2-in. baking pan. Bake at 325° for 60 minutes or until cake tests done. **Yield:** 12-15 servings.

APPLE PRALINE PIE
Bev Higley, Londonderry, Ohio

I've won a couple of first-place prizes at our county fair with this pie! See if it becomes a prize-winner at your house, too.

7 cups thinly sliced peeled baking apples
1 cup sugar
6 tablespoons all-purpose flour
1 teaspoon ground cinnamon
1 teaspoon ground nutmeg
Pastry for double-crust pie (9 inches)
3 tablespoons apple cider
2 tablespoons butter *or* margarine, melted
PRALINE TOPPING:
2 tablespoons butter *or* margarine
1/4 cup packed brown sugar
1 tablespoon light cream
2 tablespoons apple cider
1/2 cup chopped pecans

In a bowl, mix apples, sugar, flour, cinnamon and nutmeg. Line pie plate with bottom crust; brush well with apple cider. Add apple mixture; pour any remaining cider over all. Drizzle with butter. Top with second crust; flute edges to seal. Cut slits in top. Bake at 350° for 50 minutes. Meanwhile, for topping, melt butter in a small saucepan. Add brown sugar, cream and cider; slowly bring to a full rolling boil, stirring occasionally. Remove from the heat and stir in pecans. Remove pie from oven and place on a baking sheet; pour topping over pie. Return to the oven for 5-10 minutes or until topping bubbles. Cool at least 1 hour before serving. **Yield:** 8 servings.

APPLE CINNAMON PUFFS
Mary Bauer, Wichita, Kansas

When I was growing up on a farm, my mother always made homemade bread and rolls. Walking home from school, I think I could smell the bread baking a mile away! I've always liked to try new dishes...fortunately, my husband also likes to eat them! We have an apple tree, so I'm always looking for different apple recipes.

2 cups all-purpose flour, *divided*
1 package (1/4 ounce) active dry yeast
2 tablespoons sugar
1/2 teaspoon salt
3/4 cup warm water (120° to 130°)
1/4 cup vegetable oil
1 egg
1 cup chopped peeled baking apples
TOPPING:
1/4 cup sugar
1 teaspoon ground cinnamon
1/4 cup finely chopped nuts
3 tablespoons butter *or* margarine, melted

In mixing bowl, combine 1 cup flour, yeast, sugar and salt. Mix well. Add warm water, oil and egg. Blend on low speed until moistened; beat 3 minutes on medium speed.

By hand, gradually stir in remaining flour to make a soft dough. Stir in apples. Spoon into 12 well-greased muffin cups. Let rise in a warm place until doubled in size, about 30 minutes (do not cover). Bake at 375° for 20 minutes or until golden brown. For topping, combine sugar, cinnamon and nuts. Dip tops of warm puffs in melted butter, then sprinkle with sugar mixture. Serve warm. **Yield:** 1 dozen.

APPLE COFFEE CAKE BREAD
Gerry Bevins, Bristol, Tennessee

I've loved to cook since my grandmother helped me stand in a chair and "fry" toast when I was 4. I've been a nurse for 18 years, and my husband and I and our daughter recently moved here to Bristol, Tennessee from Bristol, Virginia—the state line runs down Main Street!

1 cup sugar
3/4 cup butter *or* margarine, *divided*
2 eggs
1 teaspoon baking soda
1/4 cup buttermilk
2 cups all-purpose flour
1/2 teaspoon salt
2 cups chopped peeled baking apples
1/2 cup chopped nuts
1/2 cup raisins
1/2 cup packed brown sugar
1/2 teaspoon ground cinnamon

In a mixing bowl, cream sugar and 1/2 cup butter. Add eggs, one at a time, beating well after each. Add baking soda to buttermilk; add to creamed mixture. Mix in flour and salt. Stir in apples, nuts and raisins. Pour into two greased and floured 8-in. x 4-in. x 3-in. loaf pans. Melt remaining butter; drizzle over loaves. Combine brown sugar and cinnamon; sprinkle over loaves. Bake at 350° for 45-50 minutes. Let cool in pans for 10 minutes. Turn out on a wire rack to cool. Slice in 1-1/2-in. pieces to serve. **Yield:** 2 loaves.

CARAMEL APPLE PIE
Clara Sawlaw, Paris, Illinois

I thought there must be a simpler (and less messy!) way to enjoy a caramel apple—and I was right! I developed this recipe myself, and my caramel apple-loving family approved.

2-1/2 cups shredded peeled baking apples
35 caramels
1 tablespoon water
1/4 cup butter *or* margarine, melted
1/2 cup packed brown sugar
1/2 cup light corn syrup
1/3 cup all-purpose flour
2 eggs, lightly beaten
1 cup salted peanuts, chopped
1 unbaked pie shell (9 inches)

Place apples in a strainer to drain. In the top of a double boiler, place caramels and water; heat for 10 minutes or until caramels are partially melted. Cover and set aside, keeping caramels in pan over heated water. In a small bowl, mix butter, brown sugar, corn syrup, flour and eggs. Squeeze excess moisture from apples and stir into egg mixture. Add peanuts. Add melted caramels and stir to mix. Pour into pie shell. Bake at 350° for 45 minutes or until set. **Yield:** 8-10 servings.

APPLE NUT MUFFINS

Delores Schmitt, Neillsville, Wisconsin

I added bran to a favorite apple muffin recipe I had to make it more nutritious. We enjoy these warmed for a quick breakfast.

1-1/2 cups wheat bran (Miller's Bran)
1 cup apple juice
1/2 cup vegetable oil
1 egg, beaten
1 teaspoon vanilla extract
2 cups all-purpose flour
1/4 cup sugar
1/4 cup packed brown sugar
1 tablespoon baking powder
1/2 teaspoon salt
1 baking apple, peeled and chopped
1/2 cup chopped nuts
1/2 teaspoon ground cinnamon

In a mixing bowl, combine the first five ingredients; mix well. Let stand for 10 minutes. Combine flour, sugars, baking powder and salt; add to the bran mixture. Stir well (the batter will be lumpy). Fold in apple and nuts. Spoon into 12 greased or paper-lined muffin cups (cups will be full). Sprinkle with cinnamon. Bake at 375° for 25 minutes or until muffins test done. **Yield:** 1 dozen.

APPLE GINGERBREAD

Mrs. Francis Nourse, Sheffield, Massachusetts

A slice of spicy gingerbread fresh from the oven will warm you up on a wintry day! The apples are a nice variation and really add to the flavor.

4 to 5 cups sliced peeled baking apples
1-1/2 cups sugar, *divided*
1 cup dark molasses
1/2 cup butter *or* margarine, softened
2 eggs, lightly beaten
2-1/2 cups all-purpose flour
1 teaspoon baking soda
1 teaspoon ground ginger
1 teaspoon ground cinnamon
1 teaspoon ground cloves
1/2 teaspoon salt
1/2 cup boiling water

Arrange apple slices in a greased 17-in. x 11-in. x 1-in. pan. Sprinkle with 1/2 cup sugar. Bake at 350° for 5 minutes. Remove from the oven. In a small bowl, mix remaining sugar with molasses and butter until smooth. Mix in eggs. In a large bowl, combine flour, baking soda, ginger, cinnamon, cloves and salt. Add molasses mixture and beat until

smooth. Add boiling water and mix. Pour batter over apples and spread evenly in pan. Bake for 30 minutes or until cake tests done. **Yield:** 20-24 servings.

SOUR CREAM APPLE COFFEE CAKE

Beverly Williams, Woodland, Michigan

I wish I could give credit where it's due, but I don't remember where this recipe originated. It seems as soon as this coffee cake is out of the oven, my family has it eaten!

1/2 cup butter *or* margarine, softened
1 cup sugar
2 eggs
1 teaspoon vanilla extract
2 cups all-purpose flour
1 teaspoon baking soda
1/2 teaspoon salt
1 cup (8 ounces) sour cream
1-1/2 cups chopped peeled baking apples
TOPPING:
1/2 cup packed brown sugar
1/2 cup chopped pecans
2 tablespoons butter *or* margarine, softened
1 teaspoon apple pie spice

In a mixing bowl, cream butter and sugar. Beat in eggs and vanilla. Combine flour, baking soda and salt; add alternately with sour cream to the creamed mixture. Fold in apples. Spoon into a greased 9-in. square baking pan. In a small bowl, mix topping ingredients; sprinkle over batter. Bake at 350° for 35-40 minutes or until done. **Yield:** 9 servings.

BREAKFAST APPLES

Rosemary Franta, New Ulm, Minnesota

I have handed out this recipe to more people than any other. It has a delicious nutty flavor. Use it to top waffles or pancakes...or mix with vanilla or plain yogurt for a light and quick dessert.

8 baking apples (about 3-1/2 pounds), peeled and sliced
1/2 to 1 cup chopped pecans
3/4 cup raisins
1/2 cup butter *or* margarine, melted
1/3 cup sugar
1/4 cup old-fashioned oats
2 tablespoons lemon juice
1/4 teaspoon ground cinnamon

Combine all ingredients in a slow cooker. Cook on high heat for 3 hours, stirring occasionally. Serve warm with waffles, pancakes or yogurt. **Yield:** 5 cups.

APPLE A DAY. *Clockwise from upper left: Apple Walnut Cake, Taffy Apple Salad, Apple Yeast Bread, Autumn Casserole and German Apple Pancake (all recipes on pages 76 and 77).*

APPLE WALNUT CAKE

Lynne Campbell, Lansing, Michigan

(PICTURED ON PAGE 74)

The aroma and flavor of this old-fashioned tube cake will remind you of cakes your grandma made! The apple-walnut combination makes it perfect for fall...and it can be served for breakfast, brunch or dessert.

> 1 cup butter *or* margarine, softened
> 2 cups sugar
> 3 eggs
> 2 teaspoons vanilla extract
> 3 cups all-purpose flour
> 1-1/2 teaspoons baking powder
> 1 teaspoon ground cinnamon
> 1/2 teaspoon salt
> 1/4 teaspoon ground mace
> 3 cups chopped peeled baking apples
> 2 cups chopped walnuts

In a mixing bowl, cream butter and sugar. Add eggs, one at a time, beating well after each addition. Add vanilla. Combine flour, baking powder, cinnamon, salt and mace; gradually add to creamed mixture. Stir in apples and nuts. (Batter will be very stiff.) Spoon into a greased and floured 10-in. tube pan. Bake at 325° for 1 hour and 25 minutes or until cake tests done. Cool 10 minutes in pan before removing to a wire rack to cool completely. **Yield:** 16 servings.

APPLE YEAST BREAD

Marilyn Strickland, Williamson, New York

(PICTURED ON PAGE 75)

This is one of the recipes I included in a cookbook I put together after my grown children kept calling home to ask how to make some of their favorite dishes. What a wonderful experience that was, gathering my mother's and my own recipes plus those from friends and family. My daughters and some of their friends did some artwork for it, and we now have a book we are proud to share!

> 2 tablespoons butter *or* margarine, melted
> 1/2 cup sugar
> 1 teaspoon ground cinnamon
> 1 large baking apple, peeled and thinly sliced
> 1/4 cup raisins
> 1 package (1/4 ounce) active dry yeast
> 3/4 cup warm water (110° to 115°)
> 1/4 cup sugar
> 1 teaspoon salt
> 2-1/4 cups all-purpose flour, *divided*
> 1 egg, lightly beaten
> 1/4 cup shortening

Pour butter into a 9-in. square baking pan. Mix sugar and cinnamon; sprinkle over butter. Arrange apple slices in pan. Sprinkle with raisins. In a mixing bowl, combine yeast, water, sugar, salt and 1 cup flour; beat for 1-2 minutes. Add egg, shortening and remaining flour. Beat for 1 minute. Drop dough by spoonfuls over apples. Cover and let rise in

a warm place until almost doubled, about 1 hour. Bake at 350° for 30-35 minutes or until done. Invert pan on a serving platter. **Yield:** 9 servings.

TAFFY APPLE SALAD

Cathy LaReau, Sumava Resorts, Indiana

(PICTURED ON PAGE 75)

Kids especially will eat up this salad, which really does taste like a taffy apple! My whole family enjoys it, and I hope you do, too.

> 1 can (20 ounces) crushed pineapple
> 4 cups miniature marshmallows
> 1 egg, lightly beaten
> 1/2 cup sugar
> 1/4 cup packed brown sugar
> 1 tablespoon all-purpose flour
> 1-1/2 tablespoons vinegar
> 3 cups diced unpeeled apples
> 1-1/2 cups lightly salted peanuts, coarsely chopped
> 1 carton (8 ounces) frozen whipped topping, thawed

Drain pineapple, reserving juice. In a large bowl, combine pineapple and marshmallows; cover and chill for several hours. In a saucepan, combine pineapple juice, egg, sugars, flour and vinegar; cook and stir until thickened. Remove from the heat; cool. Refrigerate. Stir into pineapple and marshmallows. Add apples, peanuts and whipped topping; blend well. Refrigerate until ready to serve. **Yield:** 10-12 servings.

GERMAN APPLE PANCAKE

Judi Van Beek, Lynden, Washington

(PICTURED ON PAGE 74)

If you're looking for a pretty dish to make when having guests for brunch, try this. Everyone I've served it to has enjoyed it...except for one time, that is, when my husband tried to make it following my recipe, which I'd written down incorrectly! If you don't leave out the flour like I did, it'll turn out terrific!

PANCAKE:
> 3 eggs
> 1 cup milk
> 3/4 cup all-purpose flour
> 1/2 teaspoon salt
> 1/8 teaspoon ground nutmeg
> 3 tablespoons butter *or* margarine

TOPPING:
> 2 tart baking apples, peeled and sliced
> 3 to 4 tablespoons butter *or* margarine
> 2 tablespoons sugar

Confectioners' sugar
Lemon wedges

Preheat oven and 10-in. cast-iron skillet to 425°. Meanwhile, place eggs, milk, flour, salt and nutmeg in a blender container; process until smooth. Add butter to skillet; return to oven until butter bubbles. Pour batter into skillet. Bake, uncovered, for 20 minutes or until pancake puffs and edges are browned and crisp. For topping, place apples, butter and sugar in a skillet; cook and stir over medium heat until apples are tender. Spoon into baked pancake. Sprinkle with confectioners' sugar. Cut and serve immediately with lemon wedges. **Yield:** 6-8 servings.

AUTUMN CASSEROLE
Shirley Brownell, Amsterdam, New York
(PICTURED ON PAGE 75)

Since our state is second in the country in apple production, I make many recipes using them. My family often requests this dish for Sunday dinners and Thanksgiving.

> 3 cups sliced unpeeled tart apples
> 3 cups sliced carrots, cooked
> 1/2 cup packed brown sugar
> 2 tablespoons all-purpose flour
> 1 teaspoon ground cinnamon
> 1/2 teaspoon salt
> 1 tablespoon butter *or* margarine
> 3/4 cup orange juice

Place half the apples in a greased 2-qt. baking dish. Cover with half the carrots. In a bowl, combine brown sugar, flour, cinnamon and salt. Cut in butter until crumbly; sprinkle half over apples and carrots. Repeat layers. Pour orange juice over all. Bake, uncovered, at 350° for 30-35 minutes. **Yield:** 6 servings.

FRESH APPLE CAKE
WITH CARAMEL SAUCE
Mrs. Karl Zank, Sand Lake, Michigan

I've had this recipe for years and make it often since Michigan has an abundance of apples. The caramel sauce is a special touch, especially when serving guests.

> 1/2 cup butter *or* margarine
> 3/4 cup sugar
> 1 egg
> 1 cup all-purpose flour
> 1/2 teaspoon baking soda
> 1/2 teaspoon ground nutmeg
> 1/2 teaspoon ground cinnamon
> 2 cups chopped peeled baking apples
> 1/2 cup chopped walnuts
CARAMEL SAUCE:
> 1/2 cup packed brown sugar
> 2 tablespoons cornstarch
> 1/2 cup light corn syrup
> 1/4 cup cream *or* evaporated milk
> 1/4 cup butter *or* margarine
> 1/4 teaspoon salt
> 1 egg, beaten

In a mixing bowl, cream butter and sugar. Beat in the egg. Combine flour, baking soda, nutmeg and cinnamon; add to creamed mixture and mix well. Stir in apples and walnuts.

Turn into a greased 8-in. square baking pan. Bake at 350° for 30-35 minutes or until cake tests done. Meanwhile, for caramel sauce, blend brown sugar and cornstarch in a saucepan. Add remaining ingredients; cook and stir until thickened, about 3 minutes. Serve cake warm or cold with warm caramel sauce. **Yield:** 9 servings.

OLD-FASHIONED
APPLE CRISP
Linda Troyer, Bellville, Ohio

My whole family loves this recipe—fortunately for me, it's a breeze to prepare!

> 6 large baking apples, peeled and sliced
> 1 cup plus 2 tablespoons sugar, *divided*
> 1-1/4 teaspoons ground cinnamon, *divided*
> 3/4 cup all-purpose flour
> 1/2 cup butter *or* margarine
> 1/2 cup water

Place apples in a greased 8-in. square baking pan. Sprinkle with 2 tablespoons sugar and 1/4 teaspoon cinnamon. In a medium bowl, combine flour and remaining sugar and cinnamon; cut in butter until crumbs form. Drizzle water over apples; sprinkle with crumb topping. Bake at 350° for 60 minutes or until apples are tender. **Yield:** 6-8 servings.

STRAWBERRY APPLE SALAD
Polly Gerber, Chicago, Illinois

Although I live in the city now, I was born and raised in the country in Wayne County, Ohio. Our county and the neighboring one, Holmes, had a high Amish population, and it is from one of my Amish friends that I received this recipe. It is traditionally served at weddings in some Amish circles.

> 1 can (20 ounces) crushed pineapple
> 1 package (6 ounces) strawberry-flavored gelatin
> 2 cups boiling water
> 2 cups diced peeled apples
> 1/2 cup sugar
> 2 tablespoons all-purpose flour
> 1 egg, beaten
> 2 tablespoons butter *or* margarine
> 4 ounces cream cheese, softened
> 1 envelope whipped topping mix, prepared
>   according to package directions

Drain pineapple, reserving juice. Set aside 1/2 cup. To remaining juice, add enough cold water to equal 2 cups. In a bowl, dissolve gelatin in boiling water; stir in the juice/water mixture. Add pineapple and apples. Pour into an oiled 13-in. x 9-in. x 2-in. pan; cover and chill until firm. In a saucepan, combine sugar and flour; gradually stir in reserved pineapple juice. Add egg and butter; cook and stir until thickened. Add cream cheese and stir until smooth. Cool. Fold in prepared whipped topping. Spread over gelatin. Cover and chill until topping is set, about 3 hours. **Yield:** 15 servings.

BERRIES

Nothing sweetens your day like a bounty of juicy berries...and these recipes will help you enjoy them even more! From tart cobblers to steaming muffins bursting with berries, why not let these colorful fruits brighten your table?

CRANBERRY-ORANGE BARS

Margaret Adelman, Bellingham, Minnesota
(PICTURED AT LEFT)

My mother has had this recipe for years. I love it! These bars make great snacks, but can also be served for dessert.

    3 cups fresh *or* frozen cranberries
    2 large unpeeled oranges, cut into quarters
      and seeded
2-1/2 cups sugar
    3 tablespoons cornstarch
    1 teaspoon ground ginger
  1/2 cup chopped nuts, optional
CRUST:
3-1/4 cups all-purpose flour
  3/4 cup sugar
    1 tablespoon grated lemon peel
    1 cup butter *or* margarine
    3 egg yolks
  3/4 teaspoon vanilla extract
    1 to 2 tablespoons water

Grind cranberries and oranges (including peel). Set aside. In a saucepan, combine sugar, cornstarch and ginger. Add ground fruit; bring to a boil. Reduce heat; cook and stir for 15 minutes or until thick. Remove from the heat; stir in nuts if desired. Set aside to cool. Meanwhile, for crust, combine flour, sugar and lemon peel in a large bowl. Cut in butter until coarse crumbs form. Add egg yolks, vanilla and just enough water so dough holds its shape. Pat two-thirds of dough into a greased 13-in. x 9-in. x 2-in. baking pan. Cover with cranberry-orange mixture. Crumble remaining dough on top. Bake at 425° for 20-25 minutes or until topping is golden brown. Cool; cut into bars. **Yield:** about 2-1/2 dozen.

FRESH STRAWBERRY PIE

Mary Egan, Carney, Michigan
(PICTURED AT LEFT AND ON COVER)

Each year we wait for "strawberry time" here in the Upper Peninsula of Michigan. We believe our strawberries are the

RIPE FOR THE PICKING. *Pictured at left, from the top: Cranberry-Orange Bars, Blueberry Muffins and Fresh Strawberry Pie (all recipes on this page).*

best in the country! After picking them at a nearby farm, I can't wait to get home to make this pie.

BOTTOM LAYER:
    2 cups sliced fresh strawberries
    1 pastry shell (9 inches), baked and cooled
MIDDLE LAYER:
    2 cups halved fresh strawberries, mashed
    1 cup sugar
    3 tablespoons cornstarch
TOP LAYER:
    2 cups halved fresh strawberries
    1 cup whipping cream
    2 tablespoons sugar
  1/4 teaspoon almond extract, optional

For bottom layer, place sliced strawberries in the pie shell. For middle layer, combine mashed strawberries, sugar and cornstarch in a saucepan. Bring to a boil; cook and stir until mixture is thick and clear. Cool and pour over bottom layer. For top layer, arrange strawberry halves on top of pie. Whip cream with sugar and almond extract if desired until stiff peaks form. Spread over pie or dollop on individual servings. Best served the same day. **Yield:** 6-8 servings.

BLUEBERRY MUFFINS

Carolyn Gilman, Westbrook, Maine
(PICTURED AT LEFT)

I prepare these muffins with the blueberries that grow wild along the rocky coast of Maine. I have worked on this recipe for several years and finally feel that I have it perfected.

  3/4 cup milk
  1/4 cup lemon juice
    2 cups all-purpose flour
  3/4 cup sugar
    1 tablespoon baking powder
  1/2 teaspoon ground cinnamon
  1/2 teaspoon salt
    1 egg, lightly beaten
  1/4 cup vegetable oil
    1 cup fresh *or* frozen blueberries

In a small bowl, mix milk and lemon juice; set aside. In a large bowl, combine flour, sugar, baking powder, cinnamon and salt. Set aside. Add egg and oil to milk mixture; mix well. Gently stir into flour mixture just until moistened. Fold in blueberries. Fill greased or paper-lined muffin cups two-thirds full. Bake at 400° for 22-24 minutes or until center of muffin springs back when lightly touched. **Yield:** 1 dozen.

RUSSIAN CREAM
Barbara Glover, Port St. Lucie, Florida

Since it's always warm in the South, we like to eat light—especially in the summer. Don't let the simplicity of this recipe fool you—Russian Cream is pure heaven.

       3/4 cup sugar
         1 envelope (1 tablespoon) unflavored gelatin
       1/2 cup cold water
         1 cup whipping cream
   1-1/2 cups (12 ounces) sour cream
         1 teaspoon vanilla extract
      4 to 5 cups fresh fruit (bite-size pieces)

In a saucepan, combine sugar and gelatin. Stir in water; let stand 5 minutes. Bring to a boil, stirring constantly. Remove from the heat; stir in whipping cream. In a bowl, combine sour cream and vanilla. Add gradually to hot mixture; mix until smooth. Pour into a 4-cup bowl or mold. Cover and chill for 4 hours or overnight. Serve over fruit. **Yield:** 8 servings.

BUTTERMILK
BLUEBERRY PANCAKES
Ann Moran, Islesford, Maine

Here's the classic blueberry pancake—light as a feather and bursting with flavor!

   2 cups buttermilk
   2 eggs, lightly beaten
   1 tablespoon vegetable oil
   2 cups all-purpose flour
   1 tablespoon sugar
   1/2 teaspoon baking soda
   1/4 teaspoon salt
   1/8 teaspoon baking powder
   1 cup fresh *or* frozen blueberries
Butter *or* margarine, optional
Syrup, optional

In a large bowl, mix buttermilk, eggs and oil. Add flour, sugar, baking soda, salt and baking powder. Stir until blended, but a few lumps remain. Pour by 1/4 cupfuls onto a hot greased griddle. Sprinkle 1 tablespoon blueberries on each pancake. Cook until bubbles form; flip and cook until browned on other side. Serve with butter and syrup if desired. **Yield:** 12-14 pancakes.

LEFTOVER EGGNOG
CRANBERRY MUFFINS
Sylvia Davis, Calgary, Alberta

I devised this recipe after Christmas one year to make use of leftover eggnog and cranberries. My friends and family have just raved about these muffins.

   3 cups all-purpose flour
   6 tablespoons sugar
   4-1/2 teaspoons baking powder

   1-1/2 teaspoons salt
   1-1/2 cups prepared eggnog
       2 eggs, lightly beaten
     1/2 cup butter *or* margarine, melted
   1-1/2 cups jellied cranberry sauce
       1 cup chopped pecans

In a large bowl, combine flour, sugar, baking powder and salt. In a small bowl, mix eggnog, eggs and butter. Stir into flour mixture just until blended. Fold in cranberry sauce and pecans. Fill greased or paper-lined muffin cups two-thirds full. Bake at 375° for 25 minutes or until center of muffin springs back when lightly touched. **Yield:** 2 dozen.

THREE-BERRY PIE WITH
CRUMB TOPPING
Jan Meinke, Parma, Ohio

I first made this pie for my family because I didn't have enough of one kind of berry. Now, I bring several of these pies to bake sales...they're often purchased before I can even get them to the sale table!

   1-1/2 cups fresh *or* frozen blueberries
   1-1/2 cups fresh *or* frozen blackberries
   1-1/2 cups fresh *or* frozen elderberries *or* raspberries
       4 tablespoons quick-cooking tapioca
       1 cup sugar
       1 tablespoon lemon juice
       1 unbaked pastry shell (9 inches)
TOPPING:
     3/4 cup all-purpose flour
     1/2 cup sugar
     1/3 cup butter *or* margarine

In a large bowl, combine berries. Add tapioca, sugar and lemon juice; toss. Spoon into pastry shell. For topping, combine flour and sugar in a medium bowl. Cut in butter until coarse crumbs form. Sprinkle over pie. Bake at 400° for 45 minutes or until bubbly. **Yield:** 6-8 servings.

FRESH 'N' FROZEN BERRIES:
Wash and dry berries thoroughly, then freeze in a single layer on a jelly roll pan. When frozen solid, pack berries in heavy freezer bags or containers. They should keep for as long as a year.

LEMON-RASPBERRY MUFFINS
Karen Paumen, Buffalo, Minnesota

My family celebrates Christmas and Easter with a really big brunch. It's getting harder and harder to find new recipes, so I made this one up. My family loves berry muffins, and these rate among our favorites.

   2 cups all-purpose flour
   1 cup sugar

1 tablespoon baking powder
1/2 teaspoon salt
2 eggs, lightly beaten
1 cup buttermilk
1/2 cup vegetable oil
1 teaspoon lemon extract
1 cup fresh *or* frozen raspberries

In a large bowl, combine flour, sugar, baking powder and salt. In a small bowl, mix eggs, buttermilk, oil and lemon extract. Stir into flour mixture just until moistened. Fold in raspberries. Fill greased or paper-lined muffin cups two-thirds full. Bake at 400° for 20-22 minutes or until center of muffin springs back when lightly touched. **Yield:** 15 muffins.

CRANBERRY SALSA

Arline Roggenbuck, Shawano, Wisconsin

Wisconsin grows an abundance of cranberries and celebrates the harvest with many cranberry festivals. I don't remember where I obtained this recipe, but it's easy, different...and good! Try it with pork or leftover turkey.

2 cups fresh *or* frozen cranberries
2 cups water
1/2 cup sugar
1/4 to 1/2 cup minced fresh cilantro *or* parsley
2 to 4 tablespoons chopped jalapeno peppers
1/4 cup finely chopped onion
2 tablespoons grated orange peel
1/2 teaspoon salt
1/4 teaspoon pepper

In a saucepan, bring cranberries and water to a boil for 2 minutes. Drain. Stir in sugar until dissolved. Add cilantro, peppers, onion, orange peel, salt and pepper. Mix well. Cool and refrigerate. **Yield:** 2 cups.

BLUEBERRY CREAM PIE

Becky Roberson, Brandon, Mississippi

A co-worker and her husband own a blueberry farm—so we have a ready supply of fresh berries in the summer. This pie is a favorite dessert.

1 cup (8 ounces) sour cream
3/4 cup sugar
2 tablespoons all-purpose flour
1 teaspoon vanilla extract
1/4 teaspoon salt
1 egg, lightly beaten
3-1/2 cups blueberries
1 unbaked pastry shell (9 inches)
TOPPING:
3 tablespoons all-purpose flour
3 tablespoons chopped pecans
1-1/2 tablespoons butter *or* margarine

In a large bowl, combine sour cream, sugar, flour, vanilla, salt and egg; stir until blended. Fold in blueberries. Pour into pie shell. Bake at 400° for 30-35 minutes or until bubbly. Remove from the oven. For topping, combine flour and

pecans in a small bowl. Cut in butter until mixture resembles coarse crumbs. Sprinkle on top of pie. Return to the oven for 10 minutes. Chill before serving. Keep refrigerated. **Yield:** 6-8 servings.

CRANBERRY STRAWBERRY SAUCE

Mary Dusing, Covington, Kentucky

This recipe was given to me by my aunt quite a few years ago. It's especially good with turkey, chicken or pork, but my family also likes it as a topping for waffles, cheesecake—even ice cream!

2 cups fresh *or* frozen cranberries
1/2 cup water
1/2 cup sugar
1 carton (10 ounces) frozen sliced strawberries in syrup

In a saucepan, combine cranberries, water and sugar. Bring to a boil, stirring until sugar is dissolved. Boil gently, uncovered, 3-4 minutes or until about half of the cranberries burst. Remove from the heat; immediately add strawberries. Let stand until strawberries are completely thawed, stirring occasionally. Refrigerate. **Yield:** 2-1/2 cups.

BLUEBERRY LEMON TEA BREAD

Donna McCrimmon, Belding, Michigan

I clipped this recipe from a magazine years ago and use it often, especially during blueberry season. The bread has a refreshing lemony tang that goes well with a cup of hot tea or coffee.

1 cup fresh *or* frozen blueberries
1-2/3 cups plus 1 tablespoon all-purpose flour, *divided*
1/2 cup butter *or* margarine, softened
1 cup sugar
2 eggs
1-1/2 teaspoons baking powder
1/4 teaspoon salt
1/2 cup milk
1 tablespoon grated lemon peel
GLAZE:
1/4 cup sugar
1/4 cup lemon juice

Toss berries with 1 tablespoon flour; set aside. In a large mixing bowl, cream butter and sugar until fluffy. Add eggs, one at a time, beating after each addition. Combine baking powder, salt and remaining flour. Add alternately with milk to creamed mixture. Fold in blueberries and lemon peel. Pour batter into a greased 9-in. x 5-in. x 3-in. loaf pan. Bake at 350° for 50-55 minutes or until bread tests done. Cool 10 minutes. Meanwhile, for glaze, combine sugar and lemon juice in a saucepan. Heat and stir until sugar is dissolved. Remove bread from pan; prick top with a toothpick. Brush hot glaze over bread. Cool completely before slicing. **Yield:** 1 loaf.

BLUEBERRY SOUR CREAM POUND CAKE

Juanita Miller, Arnett, Oklahoma

(PICTURED AT RIGHT)

I used to sell several lines of kitchenware through home parties. This recipe came from the hostess at one of those parties. It's been a favorite ever since!

> 1 cup butter *or* margarine, softened
> 3 cups sugar
> 6 eggs, *separated*
> 1 cup (8 ounces) sour cream
> 1/4 teaspoon baking soda
> 3 cups all-purpose flour
> 1 teaspoon vanilla extract
> 1 teaspoon almond extract
> 1 teaspoon butter flavoring
> 1-1/2 cups fresh *or* frozen blueberries

In a mixing bowl, cream butter; gradually add sugar and mix well. Add egg yolks, one at a time, beating well after each addition. In a separate bowl, combine sour cream and baking soda. Add alternately with the flour to creamed mixture. Beat egg whites until stiff peaks form. Fold egg whites, extracts, butter flavoring and berries into batter. Spoon into a greased 10-in. tube pan. Bake at 350° for 60-70 minutes or until cake tests done. **Yield:** 16-20 servings.

RASPBERRY CIDER

Pat McIlrath, Grinnell, Iowa

(PICTURED AT RIGHT)

Here's a refreshing cooler for a late-summer afternoon. The cider is so pretty in a clear sparkling glass!

> 1 pint (2 cups) fresh *or* frozen raspberries
> 4 cups apple cider
Mint sprigs, optional

In a bowl, crush berries. Add cider and mix well. Strain through a fine sieve or cheesecloth. Chill. Garnish with mint sprigs if desired. **Yield:** about 5 cups.

BERRY WHIRLIGIG

Pearl Stanford, Medford, Oregon

(PICTURED AT RIGHT)

I was crew cook at a lake resort for many years, and the folks really ate up this dessert to the very last berry!

> 1/2 cup sugar
> 2 tablespoons cornstarch
> 1/2 teaspoon salt
> 1/4 teaspoon ground cinnamon
> 1 cup water
> 3 cups fresh *or* frozen blackberries *or* a mixture of berries
WHIRLIGIGS:
> 1 cup all-purpose flour
> 2 teaspoons baking powder

> 1/2 teaspoon salt
> 2 tablespoons shortening
> 1 egg, lightly beaten
> 2 tablespoons milk
> 1/4 cup butter *or* margarine, softened
> 1/2 cup sugar
> 1 teaspoon grated lemon peel
> 1/4 teaspoon ground cinnamon

In a saucepan, combine sugar, cornstarch, salt and cinnamon. Add water. Cook until mixture boils and thickens. Stir in berries; cook over low heat for 5 minutes. Pour into a greased 8-in. square baking pan. Set aside. Combine flour, baking powder and salt in a bowl. Cut in shortening until coarse crumbs form. In another bowl, mix egg and milk. Add to flour mixture; mix to make a smooth dough. Knead several minutes. Roll into a 12-in. x 8-in. rectangle. Spread with butter. Combine sugar, peel and cinnamon; sprinkle over dough. Starting at a long end, roll up; seal edges. Cut into 9 slices. Place slices over berry mixture. Bake at 400° for 22-25 minutes or until golden brown. **Yield:** 9 servings.

BLUEBERRY-SAUSAGE BREAKFAST CAKE

Peggy Frazier, Indianapolis, Indiana

(PICTURED AT RIGHT)

I fix this recipe for my co-workers often. It's very simple and can be prepared the night before.

> 1/2 cup butter *or* margarine, softened
> 3/4 cup sugar
> 1/4 cup packed brown sugar
> 2 eggs
> 2 cups all-purpose flour
> 1 teaspoon baking powder
> 1/2 teaspoon baking soda
> 1 cup (8 ounces) sour cream
> 1 pound bulk pork sausage, cooked and drained
> 1 cup fresh *or* frozen blueberries
> 1/2 cup chopped pecans
BLUEBERRY SAUCE:
> 1/2 cup sugar
> 2 tablespoons cornstarch
> 1/2 cup water
> 2 cups fresh *or* frozen blueberries

In a mixing bowl, cream butter and sugars. Add eggs, one at a time, beating well after each addition. Combine flour, baking powder and baking soda; add alternately with sour cream to creamed mixture, beating well after each addition. Fold in sausage and blueberries. Pour into a greased 13-in. x 9-in. x 2-in. baking pan. Sprinkle with pecans. Bake at 350° for 35-40 minutes or until cake tests done. For sauce, combine sugar and cornstarch in a saucepan. Add water and blueberries. Cook and stir until thick and bubbly. Spoon over individual servings. **Yield:** 9-12 servings.

BERRY GOOD! *Pictured at right, clockwise from top: Blueberry Sour Cream Pound Cake, Raspberry Cider, Berry Whirligig and Blueberry-Sausage Breakfast Cake (all recipes on this page).*

...RIES, ADD CIDER
...E SIEVE OR
...E WITH
BERRY WHIRLIGIG
...UGAR
...OONS CORNSTARCH
...N SALT
...N CINNAMON
...ER
...KBERRIES OR A MIXTURE OF BERRIES
...URPOSE FLOUR
...BAKING POWDER
...ALT
...NS SHORTENING
...TLY BEATEN
...S MILK

RASPBERRY MUFFINS
Pamela MacNutt, Oakham, Massachusetts

This was originally a blueberry muffin recipe, but since raspberries grow like crazy around here, I tried them instead. They worked great!

```
1-3/4 cups all-purpose flour
    2 teaspoons baking powder
  1/3 cup shortening
    1 cup sugar
    2 eggs, lightly beaten
  1/2 cup milk
    1 teaspoon vanilla extract
    1 to 2 cups fresh or frozen raspberries
Additional sugar
```

Combine flour and baking powder; set aside. In a large mixing bowl, cream shortening and sugar. Add eggs; mix well. Combine milk and vanilla; add to creamed mixture alternately with flour mixture. Fold in the raspberries. Fill greased or paper-lined muffin cups two-thirds full. Sprinkle with sugar. Bake at 375° for 20-25 minutes or until center of muffin springs back when lightly touched. **Yield:** about 1 dozen.

OZARK BLUE-CRANBERRY PIE
Mary Marso, Crocker, Missouri

Here in the Missouri Ozarks, my daughter and I pick blueberries at a nearby Amish farm and freeze them for year-round use. I got this recipe from a local newspaper.

CRUST:
```
    2 cups all-purpose flour
    1 teaspoon salt
  1/2 teaspoon ground nutmeg
  2/3 cup plus 2 tablespoons shortening, chilled
    4 to 5 tablespoons ice water
```
FILLING:
```
    1 can (16 ounces) whole-berry cranberry sauce
  1/3 cup packed brown sugar
  1/4 cup sugar
    2 tablespoons all-purpose flour
    2 tablespoons cornstarch
    2 tablespoons orange juice
  1/2 teaspoon grated orange peel
  1/8 teaspoon salt
    2 cups fresh or frozen blueberries
    2 tablespoons butter or margarine
```

For crust, combine flour, salt and nutmeg in a large bowl. Cut in shortening until mixture forms coarse crumbs. Add water, 1 tablespoon at a time, until ingredients are just moistened. Divide dough in half. Between sheets of waxed paper, roll each half into a circle large enough to fit a 9-in. pie pan. Press one circle into the pan; set aside the second circle. For filling, combine cranberry sauce, sugars, flour, cornstarch, orange juice, orange peel and salt in a large bowl. Mix well. Stir in blueberries. Spoon filling into pie crust; dot with butter. Place second crust over filling. Flute

edges and cut slits to vent steam. Bake at 400° for 40 minutes or until center is bubbly and crust is golden brown. Cool to room temperature before serving. **Yield:** 6-8 servings.

STRAWBERRY ALMONDINE
Robin Perry, Seneca, Pennsylvania

Strawberries are plentiful in this area in early summer. I developed this recipe to use up some berries that had been in my refrigerator for a few days. My family just loves it!

```
1-1/3 cups graham cracker crumbs
  1/2 cup confectioners' sugar
  1/4 cup melted butter or margarine
    2 packages (8 ounces each) cream cheese, softened
    1 cup sugar
    1 teaspoon vanilla extract
    1 cup sliced fresh or frozen strawberries
    1 carton (8 ounces) frozen whipped topping, thawed
  1/2 cup chopped almonds, toasted
```

In a bowl, combine graham cracker crumbs, confectioners' sugar and butter. Spread on the bottom of a 13-in. x 9-in. x 2-in. baking pan. Bake at 350° for 8 minutes. Cool. In a mixing bowl, beat cream cheese, sugar, vanilla and strawberries until smooth. Spread over cooled crust and chill until firm. Spread whipped topping over strawberry mixture and sprinkle with almonds. Cover and refrigerate at least 3 hours. **Yield:** 16-20 servings.

BLUEBERRY COFFEE CAKE
Debra Young, Winnipeg, Manitoba

My mother has been making this coffee cake for years. It is a delicate, moist cake that is not overly sweet. It's perfect with a cup of coffee in the morning!

```
  1/4 cup shortening
  3/4 cup plus 1 tablespoon sugar, divided
    1 egg, lightly beaten
    1 teaspoon vanilla extract
  3/4 cup milk
1-3/4 cups all-purpose flour
    1 tablespoon baking powder
  1/2 teaspoon salt
1-1/2 cups fresh or frozen blueberries
```
TOPPING:
```
  1/2 cup all-purpose flour
  1/4 cup packed brown sugar
  1/4 cup butter or margarine
```

In a large mixing bowl, cream shortening and 1/2 cup sugar. Add egg, vanilla and milk; mix well. Combine flour, baking powder and salt; add to creamed mixture and mix well. Spread half of the batter into a greased 9-in. springform pan. Spoon berries over batter. Sprinkle with remaining sugar. Cover with remaining batter. For topping, combine flour and brown sugar in a small bowl. Cut in butter until mixture forms coarse crumbs. Sprinkle over batter. Bake at 375° for 35-40 minutes or until cake tests done. **Yield:** 8-10 servings.

SCHAUM TORTE
Patricia Gantz, Wauwatosa, Wisconsin

Before the days of automatic mixers, this recipe involved long and tiresome beating. Many times, husbands were drafted to help when the tired arms of the wife gave out. But nowadays, Schaum Torte is a breeze to prepare.

    6 egg whites
1/4 teaspoon cream of tartar
    2 cups sugar
    1 teaspoon vanilla extract
    1 teaspoon vinegar
    1 pint vanilla ice cream
    1 pint fresh strawberries, hulled, sliced and
      sweetened
    1 cup heavy cream, whipped

In mixing bowl, beat egg whites until foamy. Add cream of tartar; continue beating until soft peaks form. Gradually add sugar, 1 tablespoon at a time, beating until mixture is stiff and glossy. Add vanilla and vinegar; mix well. Spread batter in a greased 10-in. springform pan. Bake at 275° for 1 hour. Turn oven off; let torte cool in oven. With a sharp knife, cut around edges of pan; turn torte onto a platter. Serve with ice cream, strawberries and whipped cream. **Yield:** 8-10 servings.

SPEEDY BLUEBERRY REFRIGERATOR JAM
Janet Schmitt, Apex, North Carolina

This recipe is one of my favorites because it is simple...and always turns out delicious!

    4 cups fresh *or* frozen blueberries
    2 cups sugar
    1 package (3 ounces) lemon-flavored gelatin

In a large saucepan, combine all three ingredients. Bring to a boil. Cook and stir for 2 minutes. Pour into jars; refrigerate. **Yield:** 3 cups.

BIG DUTCH PANCAKE WITH LITTLE BERRIES
Debbie Johanesen, Missoula, Montana

This is a really fun recipe to prepare because the pancake puffs up into unique shapes. The custard-like texture and buttery flavor make it fun to eat, too!

    1 cup halved strawberries
    1 cup fresh *or* frozen raspberries
    1 cup fresh *or* frozen blackberries *or* boysenberries
1/4 cup butter *or* margarine
    1 cup milk
    4 eggs, lightly beaten
1/2 teaspoon vanilla extract
    1 cup all-purpose flour
    2 tablespoons sugar

Confectioners' sugar

In a bowl, combine berries; set aside. Cut butter into pats and place in an 8-in. square baking pan. Put pan in a 425° oven for 2 minutes or until butter melts and pan is very hot. Combine milk, eggs and vanilla in a bowl. Stir in flour and sugar; beat until well mixed. Pour into hot pan. Bake for 18-20 minutes or until puffed and brown on top. Spoon berries over top and dust with confectioners' sugar. Serve immediately. **Yield:** 6 servings.

PEACH AND BLUEBERRY CASSEROLE
Phil Byers, Kalamazoo, Michigan

This recipe uses fruits that are grown locally and available fresh at the same time of year. Try serving this "casserole" with vanilla ice cream—it's mmm-good!

    6 cups sliced fresh *or* frozen peaches (about 6 large)
    2 cups fresh *or* frozen blueberries
3/4 cup sugar, *divided*
    1 cup all-purpose flour
    1 teaspoon baking powder
1/2 teaspoon salt
    1 egg, lightly beaten
    5 tablespoons butter *or* margarine, melted
TOPPING:
3/4 teaspoon sugar
3/4 teaspoon ground cinnamon

Place peaches in a greased 2-qt. casserole. Top with blueberries. Sprinkle with 2 tablespoons of sugar. Set aside. In a medium bowl, combine flour, baking powder, salt and remaining sugar. Add egg and cut into flour mixture until coarse crumbs form. Sprinkle over fruit. Drizzle melted butter over all. Combine topping ingredients; sprinkle on top. Bake at 375° for 20 minutes. Increase oven temperature to 400° and bake an additional 12-15 minutes or until lightly browned. **Yield:** 6-8 servings.

BLUEBERRY-PEACH COBBLER
Kim McDermott, Charleston, South Carolina

This mouth-watering cobbler combines the delicious taste of low-country South Carolina blueberries with the wonderful peaches from upstate.

2-1/2 cups fresh *or* frozen blueberries
2-1/2 cups fresh *or* frozen sliced peaches
1-1/2 teaspoons lemon juice
    3/4 cup quick-cooking oats
    1/3 cup all-purpose flour
    1/3 cup packed brown sugar
      4 tablespoons butter *or* margarine

In a bowl, toss blueberries and peaches with lemon juice. Place in a greased 8-in. square baking pan. In a small bowl, mix oats, flour and brown sugar. Cut in butter until coarse crumbs form. Sprinkle over fruit. Bake at 375° for 40-45 minutes or until cobbler is bubbly and topping is golden brown. **Yield:** 8 servings

RHUBARB

*You won't have to stalk for compliments when you use this
perennial vegetable in the delightful dishes that follow.
Spring into some great eating with some tart tasty rhubarb today!*

CHERRY RHUBARB COFFEE CAKE

Kenneth Jacques, Hemet, California
(PICTURED AT LEFT)

*I'm retired now, but when I was working I made this coffee
cake for co-workers and also a men's Bible study class. I
changed the original recipe from a strawberry/rhubarb
combination to one with cherry, which I think gives it a
richer flavor.*

> 4 cups chopped fresh *or* frozen rhubarb
> 2 tablespoons lemon juice
> 1 cup sugar
> 1/3 cup cornstarch
> 1 can (20 ounces) cherry pie filling

CAKE:
> 3 cups all-purpose flour
> 1 cup sugar
> 1 teaspoon baking powder
> 1 teaspoon baking soda
> 1/2 teaspoon salt
> 1 cup butter *or* margarine
> 1 cup buttermilk
> 2 eggs, lightly beaten
> 1 teaspoon vanilla extract

CRUMB TOPPING:
> 1-1/2 cups sugar
> 1 cup all-purpose flour
> 1/2 cup butter *or* margarine

In a saucepan, cook rhubarb and lemon juice over medium-
low heat for 5 minutes, stirring often to prevent burning.
Combine sugar and cornstarch; add to rhubarb mixture. Cook
and stir 5 minutes more until thickened and bubbly. Stir in pie
filling; set aside to cool. For cake, combine flour, sugar, baking powder, baking soda and salt in a large bowl. Cut in butter until mixture resembles fine crumbs. In a mixing bowl,
beat buttermilk, eggs and vanilla. Add to flour mixture; stir
just until moistened. Spread a little more than half of the batter into a greased 13-in. x 9-in. x 2-in. baking pan. Spread
cooled filling over batter. Drop remaining batter by teaspoonfuls onto filling. For topping, combine sugar and flour. Cut in

---

THE ART OF TART. *At left, clockwise from bottom:
Rhubarb Meringue Pie, Cherry Rhubarb Coffee Cake
(recipes on this page) and Stewed Rhubarb (recipe on
page 88).*

---

butter until mixture forms coarse crumbs. Sprinkle over batter. Bake at 350° for 40-45 minutes. **Yield:** 16-20 servings.

RHUBARB MERINGUE PIE

Theresa Connell, Puyallup, Washington
(PICTURED AT LEFT)

*My husband and brother, former "rhubarb haters", now
can't wait for the first stalks of that plant to appear, herald-
ing spring and their favorite pie!*

CRUST:
> 1/2 cup butter *or* margarine, softened
> 1/4 cup sugar
> 1 teaspoon vanilla extract
> 1/2 teaspoon salt
> 1 cup all-purpose flour
> 3/4 cup quick-cooking oats

FILLING:
> 3 cups diced fresh rhubarb
> 1 tablespoon water
> 1 cup sugar
> 2 tablespoons all-purpose flour
> 1/8 teaspoon salt
> 3 eggs yolks, beaten

MERINGUE:
> 3 egg whites
> 1/8 teaspoon salt
> 1/3 cup sugar
> 1/2 teaspoon vanilla extract

For crust, cream butter, sugar, vanilla and salt in a mixing
bowl. Add flour and oats; mix well. Press over the bottom
and sides of a 9-in. pie plate. Chill while preparing filling.
Combine rhubarb and water in a saucepan. Bring to a boil,
stirring constantly. Combine sugar, flour and salt; add to the
rhubarb mixture. Bring to a boil, stirring constantly. Remove
from the heat. Add a small amount of the rhubarb mixture to
the egg yolks; mix well. Return to the pan and mix well.
Pour filling into crust. Bake at 375° for 25-30 minutes. For
meringue, beat egg whites and salt in a mixing bowl until
soft peaks form. Gradually add sugar, beating until stiff
peaks form. Stir in vanilla. Spread over hot filling. Return to
the oven for 8-10 minutes or until meringue peaks are golden
brown. Cool. Refrigerate until serving. **Yield:** 6-8 servings.

STEWED RHUBARB

Caroline Simpson, Fredericton, New Brunswick
(PICTURED ON PAGE 86)

This is my husband's favorite way to enjoy rhubarb. He has it for breakfast over his cereal or for dessert, either plain or over ice cream.

5 to 6 cups chopped fresh *or* frozen rhubarb
1 cup water
2 cups sugar
1/2 teaspoon ground cinnamon

In a saucepan, bring rhubarb and water to a full rolling boil. Add sugar and cinnamon; return to a boil. Reduce heat and simmer 10-15 minutes or until sauce reaches desired consistency. Cool. **Yield:** 5 cups.

RHUBARB FLIP

Cathy Sudbeck, Hartington, Nebraska

This rhubarb dessert is a welcome change from rhubarb pies, which seem to be so commonly served. It's light, sweet and great for that coffee break!

5 cups diced fresh *or* frozen rhubarb
1/4 cup cornstarch
5 tablespoons water
1-1/2 cups sugar
2 to 4 drops red food coloring
2 cups dry white *or* yellow cake mix
3/4 cup shredded coconut
1/2 cup chopped walnuts
1/2 cup butter *or* margarine, melted

Place rhubarb in a greased 13-in. x 9-in. x 2-in. baking pan. In a small saucepan, mix cornstarch and water; add sugar. Cook over medium heat, stirring constantly, just until mixture boils and thickens. Add food coloring. Cool slightly and pour over rhubarb. Sprinkle cake mix over rhubarb; top with coconut and nuts. Drizzle with butter. Bake at 350° for 50-55 minutes or until cake tests done. **Yield:** 12 servings.

RHUBARB SALAD

Carol Anne Janzen, Kentville, Nova Scotia

Even people who don't like rhubarb have fallen for this dish! The deceptively simple-sounding recipe does not prepare you for the delicious flavor of the finished product. With its sweet-tart flavor, it's a lovely addition to a traditional festive dinner or a buffet supper.

4 cups diced fresh *or* frozen rhubarb
1-1/2 cups cold water, *divided*
3/4 cup sugar
1 package (6 ounces) raspberry- *or* strawberry-flavored gelatin
1 tablespoon grated orange peel
1/2 cup finely chopped celery
1/2 cup chopped nuts, optional

In a saucepan, cook rhubarb, 1/2 cup water and sugar until a sauce forms, about 8 minutes. Remove from the heat; add gelatin and stir until dissolved. Add orange peel, celery, nuts if desired and remaining water; mix well. Pour into a lightly greased 4- to 5-1/2-cup mold. Cover and chill until set. **Yield:** 8 servings.

RHUBARB BERRY PIE

Mrs. Bill Lawson, Tacoma, Washington

The ingredients in this pie are abundant in this area of the country. Our valley is famous for its fields of berries as well as for rhubarb. I'm always delighted to share this favorite recipe of ours with rhubarb and berry lovers!

3 cups diced fresh *or* frozen rhubarb
1 cup fresh raspberries *or* strawberries
1-1/3 cups sugar
3 tablespoons tapioca
1 tablespoon all-purpose flour
1/2 teaspoon lemon juice
1/8 teaspoon almond extract
1/8 teaspoon ground nutmeg
1/8 teaspoon salt
Pastry for double-crust pie (9 inches)
1 tablespoon butter *or* margarine

In a bowl, combine first nine ingredients and allow to stand 15 minutes. Pour into pastry-lined pie plate. Dot with butter; cover with top crust. Cut slits in top crust. Bake at 425° for 15 minutes. Reduce heat to 350°; bake 30-35 minutes longer. **Yield:** 8 servings.

GRANDMA'S SPRING AND SUMMER TORTE

Barbara Frye, Burnsville, Minnesota

This easy-to-make torte is a wonderfully light dessert and its tart and sweet taste is delicious. I make it often for potlucks and everyone seems to enjoy it.

CRUST:
2 cups all-purpose flour
3 tablespoons sugar
1/4 teaspoon salt
1 cup butter *or* margarine, softened
2 egg yolks
1 teaspoon vanilla extract
FILLING:
1-1/2 cups sugar
1/4 cup all-purpose flour
4 cups sliced fresh *or* frozen rhubarb
1 cup light cream *or* evaporated milk
4 egg yolks, lightly beaten
2 tablespoons butter *or* margarine, softened
MERINGUE:
4 egg whites
1/4 teaspoon cream of tartar
1/2 cup sugar

For crust, combine flour, sugar and salt in a medium bowl. Cut in butter, egg yolks and vanilla until crumbly. Press mixture into the bottom of 13-in. x 9-in. x 2-in. baking pan. Combine all filling ingredients and pour over crust. Bake at 375° for 45-50 minutes or until filling is set. Meanwhile, in a mixing bowl, beat egg whites and cream of tartar until soft peaks form. Gradually add sugar, beating until stiff and glossy. Spread over filling and return to the oven for 10-12 minutes or until meringue is lightly browned. **Yield:** 15 servings.

RHUBARB COBBLER WITH OAT DUMPLINGS
Esther Yoder, Hartville, Ohio

My friend shared this recipe with me and we consider it one of our health-minded recipes. It's easy to put together, looks lovely and tastes delicious!

    3/4 cup sugar
    2 tablespoons cornstarch
    1 cup water
    1/2 cup orange juice
    4 cups sliced fresh *or* frozen rhubarb
DUMPLINGS:
    1/2 cup all-purpose flour
    1/4 cup whole wheat flour
    1/4 cup quick-cooking oats
    1-1/2 teaspoons baking powder
    1/4 teaspoon salt
    1/2 cup milk
    2 tablespoons vegetable oil
TOPPING:
    1 tablespoon sugar
    1/4 teaspoon ground cinnamon

In a saucepan, combine sugar and cornstarch. Gradually stir in water and orange juice. Cook and stir until thickened and clear. Add rhubarb and bring to a boil. Remove from the heat. Pour into a 2-qt. baking dish. For dumplings, combine flours, oats, baking powder and salt in a bowl. Combine milk and oil; add to flour mixture, stirring lightly until blended. Spoon over rhubarb. Combine topping ingredients; sprinkle over dumplings. Bake at 425° for 40 minutes. **Yield:** 8 servings.

RHUBARB PUDDING CAKE
Mindy Moeller, Boone, Iowa

I received this recipe years ago from a co-worker. Today, my family and I really enjoy this dessert. It's nice for any occasion.

    3 to 4 cups diced fresh *or* frozen rhubarb
    1 cup all-purpose flour
    3/4 cup sugar
    1/3 cup milk
    3 tablespoons butter *or* margarine, melted
    1 teaspoon baking powder
    1/4 teaspoon salt
    1/4 teaspoon vanilla extract

TOPPING:
    1 cup sugar
    1 tablespoon cornstarch
    1 cup boiling water
    1/2 teaspoon ground cinnamon

Place rhubarb in a greased 8-in. square baking pan. In a small bowl, mix flour, sugar, milk, butter, baking powder, salt and vanilla (mixture will be stiff). Spread over rhubarb. For topping, combine sugar and cornstarch. Sprinkle over dough. Pour water over all; do not stir. Sprinkle cinnamon on top. Bake at 350° for 55-65 minutes or until pudding tests done. **Yield:** 9 servings.

BAKED RHUBARB
Dorothy Anderson, Ottawa, Kansas

This warm rhubarb dish is a wonderful accompaniment for any meal. It is so flavorful for a dish that's exceptionally quick and easy to fix.

    4 cups fresh *or* frozen diced rhubarb
    4 cups cubed bread
    1-1/2 cups sugar
    1/2 cup butter *or* margarine, melted

In a bowl, combine rhubarb, bread cubes and sugar; toss to coat. Add butter; mix well. Turn into a 11-in. x 7-in. x 2-in. baking pan. Bake at 350° for 40-45 minutes or until golden. Serve warm. **Yield:** 6 servings.

RHUBARB BEEF
Bertha Davis, Springfield, Missouri

My daughter made a trip around the world and brought home this recipe from Iran. I've served it often to many of my friends and they always seem to savor its different, zingy taste.

    2 to 2-1/2 pounds beef stew meat, cut into 1-inch
        cubes
    2 tablespoons butter *or* margarine
    2 large onions, chopped
    1 teaspoon saffron
    1 can (10-1/2 ounces) beef broth
    1 cup water
    1/4 cup lemon juice
    1/4 cup chopped fresh parsley
    1-1/2 teaspoons dried mint
    2 teaspoons salt
    1/4 teaspoon pepper
    2 to 3 cups sliced fresh *or* frozen rhubarb
Hot cooked rice

In a Dutch oven, brown beef in butter. Remove meat from pan; drain all but 2 tablespoons drippings. Saute onions until lightly browned. Return meat to pan. Add saffron, broth, water, lemon juice, parsley, mint, salt and pepper; cover and simmer until meat is tender, about 2 hours. Add additional water as needed. Add rhubarb during the last 15 minutes of cooking. Serve over rice. **Yield:** 6 servings

RHUBARB COCONUT COOKIES

Betty Claycomb, Alverton, Pennsylvania
(PICTURED AT RIGHT)

At our garden club fund-raiser, each group within the club serves a different kind of food. These cookies are made by the "rhubarb group"...and they are always the first to sell out!

- 1/2 cup shortening
- 1-1/3 cups packed brown sugar
- 1 egg
- 2 cups all-purpose flour
- 1/2 teaspoon baking soda
- 1 teaspoon ground cinnamon
- 1/2 teaspoon ground cloves
- 1/2 teaspoon ground nutmeg
- 1/2 teaspoon salt
- 1/4 cup milk
- 1 cup finely diced fresh rhubarb
- 1 cup chopped pecans *or* walnuts
- 1 cup raisins
- 1/2 cup flaked coconut

In a mixing bowl, cream shortening and brown sugar. Add egg; beat well. Combine dry ingredients; add to the creamed mixture alternately with milk. Mix well. Stir in rhubarb, nuts, raisins and coconut. Drop by tablespoonfuls onto greased baking sheets. Bake at 375° for 12-15 minutes or until golden. Cool on wire racks. **Yield:** 3 dozen.

RHUBARB MARMALADE

Leo Nerbonne, Delta Junction, Alaska
(PICTURED AT RIGHT)

My daughter makes this marmalade every spring when rhubarb's abundant. Our family enjoys her gift...a refreshing departure in flavor from all the "berry" jams and jellies.

- 6 cups chopped fresh *or* frozen rhubarb
- 6 cups sugar
- 2 medium oranges

Combine rhubarb and sugar in a large heavy saucepan. Grind oranges, including the peels, in a food processor; add to rhubarb mixture. Bring to a boil. Reduce heat and simmer, uncovered, stirring often until marmalade sheets from a spoon, about 1 hour. Pour into hot jars, leaving 1/4-in. headspace. Adjust caps. Process in a boiling-water bath for 10 minutes. **Yield:** about 8 half-pints.

RHUBARB CRUMB CAKE

John Kosmas, Minneapolis, Minnesota
(PICTURED AT RIGHT)

When the rhubarb comes up, I'm the first one in our household to get at it. I treat my family to this cake every spring.

- 1/2 cup shortening
- 1-1/2 cups packed brown sugar
- 1 egg
- 1 teaspoon vanilla extract
- 2 cups all-purpose flour
- 1/2 teaspoon baking soda
- 1/4 teaspoon salt
- 1 tablespoon orange-flavored breakfast drink mix, optional
- 1 cup sour milk
- 2 cups finely chopped fresh *or* frozen rhubarb

TOPPING:

- 1/2 cup sugar
- 1 teaspoon ground cinnamon
- 1/2 cup flaked coconut
- 1/2 cup chopped nuts

In a mixing bowl, cream shortening and brown sugar. Beat in egg and vanilla. Combine flour, baking soda, salt and orange drink if desired; add to creamed mixture alternately with sour milk. Fold in rhubarb. Spread into a greased 13-in. x 9-in. x 2-in. baking pan. For topping, combine sugar and cinnamon; stir in coconut and nuts. Sprinkle over batter. Bake at 350° for 35-40 minutes. **Yield:** 12-16 servings.

RHUBARB PEACH COBBLER

Germaine Stank, Pound, Wisconsin
(PICTURED AT RIGHT)

As soon as my rhubarb plants are big enough in spring, I make this dessert. After I added the peaches, it became a standard at our house.

- 1/2 cup sugar
- 2 tablespoons cornstarch
- 3/4 teaspoon ground cinnamon
- 1/8 teaspoon salt
- 1 can (16 ounces) sliced peaches
- 3 cups sliced fresh *or* frozen rhubarb
- 1 teaspoon vanilla extract

DOUGH:

- 1-1/2 cups all-purpose flour
- 3 tablespoons sugar
- 2 teaspoons baking powder
- 1/4 teaspoon baking soda
- 1/2 teaspoon salt
- 1/4 cup butter *or* margarine
- 1 cup plain yogurt
- 1 teaspoon vanilla extract

In a large saucepan, combine sugar, cornstarch, cinnamon and salt. Drain peaches, reserving syrup. Add syrup and rhubarb to saucepan; mix well. Bring to a boil; cook and stir 2 minutes. Add peaches and vanilla. Pour into an ungreased 2-1/2-qt. baking dish; set aside. Combine flour, sugar, baking powder, baking soda and salt in a bowl. Cut in butter until mixture resembles coarse crumbs. Stir in yogurt and vanilla just until combined. Drop by tablespoons onto hot fruit. Bake, uncovered, at 400° for 30 minutes. Serve warm. **Yield:** 8 servings.

RAVES FOR RHUBARB. *Pictured at right, clockwise from top right: Rhubarb Coconut Cookies, Rhubarb Crumb Cake, Rhubarb Marmalade and Rhubarb Peach Cobbler (all recipes on this page).*

RHUBARB PUDDING
Alma Jacklin, New Durham, New Hampshire

In New England, come April and May, we can see rhubarb growing alongside almost every barn. When I was a child, I remember I would pick a stalk and chew on it. One of my neighbors gave me this recipe years ago.

4 cups diced fresh *or* frozen rhubarb
1-1/2 cups sugar, *divided*
1/4 cup water
2 tablespoons butter *or* margarine
1 cup all-purpose flour
2 teaspoons baking powder
1/2 teaspoon salt
1 cup milk
TOPPING:
1 tablespoon sugar
1 tablespoon brown sugar
1/4 teaspoon ground cinnamon

In a saucepan, cook rhubarb, 1 cup sugar, water and butter until a sauce forms, about 7-8 minutes. Pour into a greased 11-in. x 7-in. x 2-in. baking pan. In a medium bowl, combine flour, baking powder, salt and remaining sugar. Add milk and stir until smooth. Pour over rhubarb. Combine topping ingredients; sprinkle on top. Bake at 350° for 40 minutes. **Yield:** 6-8 servings.

CREAMY RHUBARB DESSERT
Gwen Hanson, Lake Mills, Wisconsin

This dessert is a longtime favorite of family and friends who eagerly await the rhubarb season. The subtle flavors of the pudding and whipped cream really soften the tart taste of the rhubarb!

4 tablespoons cornstarch
1-1/2 cups sugar
3/4 cup water
6 cups sliced fresh *or* frozen rhubarb
CRUST:
2 cups all-purpose flour
2 tablespoons confectioners' sugar
1/2 cup chopped nuts, toasted
1 cup butter *or* margarine
TOPPING:
2 cups (1 pint) whipping cream
1-1/2 cups miniature marshmallows
1 package (3.4 ounces) instant vanilla pudding mix
1-2/3 cups cold milk
1/2 cup chopped nuts, toasted, optional

In a large saucepan, mix cornstarch and sugar; stir in water until smooth. Add rhubarb; cook and stir until tender, about 10 minutes. Cool. Meanwhile, for crust, combine flour, sugar and nuts in a medium bowl. Cut in butter until coarse crumbs form. Press onto the bottom of an ungreased 13-in. x 9-in. x 2-in. baking pan. Bake at 350° for about 20 minutes or until lightly browned. Cool. Pour cooled filling over crust. Whip cream; fold in marshmallows and spread over filling. Combine pudding mix and milk; beat until slightly thickened. Spread over marshmallow topping. If desired, sprinkle with nuts. Cover and chill for several hours. **Yield:** 15 servings.

RHUBARB KETCHUP
Faith McLillan, Rawdon, Quebec

I received this recipe from a friend about 15 years ago. It's a nice surprise for ketchup lovers, and so easy to prepare. The spicy flavor makes this one of the tastiest ketchups I've ever had!

4 cups diced fresh *or* frozen rhubarb
3 medium onions, chopped
1 cup white vinegar
1 cup packed brown sugar
1 cup sugar
1 can (28 ounces) tomatoes with liquid, cut up
2 teaspoons salt
1 teaspoon ground cinnamon
1 tablespoon pickling spice

In a large saucepan, combine all ingredients. Cook for 1 hour or until thick. Cool. Refrigerate in covered containers. **Yield:** 6-7 cups.

RHUBARB PUNCH
Patty Hamm, Kuna, Idaho

This is a lively new twist on lemonade and a fun way to use up some of your extra rhubarb. We always look forward to summer when we can enjoy this refreshing drink out on our patio on a hot afternoon.

1 pound fresh *or* frozen rhubarb, chopped
1 cup water
1/2 cup sugar
1 can (6 ounces) frozen pink lemonade concentrate, thawed
1 bottle (1 liter) lemon-lime soda

In a large saucepan, combine rhubarb, water and sugar. Bring to a boil; reduce heat and simmer 5-10 minutes or until rhubarb is tender. Cool slightly. In a blender, process half the mixture at a time until smooth. Combine all ingredients in a large container; add enough water to make 1 gallon. Serve on ice. **Yield:** about 24-30 servings.

RHUBARB MUFFINS
Martha Donley, Centerville, Ohio

Since I collect muffin recipes as well as rhubarb recipes, this one was a real find! These muffins are good either for breakfast with butter or as a dessert topped with whipped cream.

- 1-1/4 cups packed brown sugar
- 1/2 cup vegetable oil
- 2 teaspoons vanilla extract
- 1 egg
- 1 cup buttermilk
- 2-1/2 cups all-purpose flour
- 1/2 teaspoon salt
- 1-1/2 cups diced fresh rhubarb
- 1 teaspoon baking soda
- 1 teaspoon baking powder
- 1/2 cup chopped nuts

TOPPING:
- 1 teaspoon ground cinnamon
- 1 tablespoon butter *or* margarine, softened
- 1/3 cup sugar

In a bowl, combine first five ingredients; mix well. Stir in flour, salt, rhubarb, baking soda, baking powder and nuts. Pour into greased or paper-lined muffin cups. Mix topping ingredients; sprinkle over muffins and press lightly into batter. Bake at 375° for 15-18 minutes. **Yield:** 15 muffins.

RASPBERRY RHUBARB JAM
LaVonne Van Hoff, Rockwell City, Iowa

I love making and enjoying this jam, but I usually end up giving most of it away! It's always a well-received gift.

- 6 cups sliced fresh *or* frozen rhubarb
- 4 cups sugar
- 1 package (6 ounces) raspberry-flavored gelatin
- 1 can (21 ounces) raspberry pie filling

Combine rhubarb and sugar in a saucepan; cover and let stand overnight. The next day, simmer, uncovered, until rhubarb is tender, about 30 minutes. Stir in gelatin and pie filling. Bring to a boil. Remove from the heat; cool. Pack in containers and refrigerate or freeze until ready to serve. **Yield:** 3 pints.

RHUBARB STEAK SAUCE
Rose Mundle, Gleichen, Alberta

When the aroma of this sauce cooking wafts through the house, my family can't wait to grill steaks! I freeze this sauce in plastic containers, and keep some refrigerated in salad dressing bottles, ready for use. I not only use it on meat, but I'll also add a dash or two to some soup recipes.

- 8 cups chopped fresh *or* frozen rhubarb
- 4 cups chopped onion
- 2 cups vinegar
- 2-1/3 cups packed brown sugar

- 1 teaspoon ground cinnamon
- 1 teaspoon ground allspice
- 1/2 teaspoon ground cloves
- 1 teaspoon salt
- 1/2 teaspoon pepper

In a large saucepan or Dutch oven, combine all ingredients. Bring to a boil. Reduce heat and simmer for 1 hour or until thickened, stirring occasionally. Cool. Refrigerate in covered containers. **Yield:** about 7 cups.

RHUBARB RELISH
Helen Brooks, Lacombe, Alberta

I remember eating this relish at my grandmother's over 50 years ago. My mother made it for years and now my daughters make it. It complements any meat, but I find it a "must" with meat loaf.

- 12 cups finely chopped fresh *or* frozen rhubarb
- 1 medium onion, chopped
- 2 cups sugar
- 1 cup cider vinegar
- 1 teaspoon salt
- 1 teaspoon ground cloves
- 1 teaspoon ground allspice
- 1/4 teaspoon paprika
- 1 teaspoon ground cinnamon

In a large saucepan, combine all ingredients. Bring to a boil. Reduce heat and simmer for about 2 hours or until mixture thickens, stirring occasionally. Pour into jars. Refrigerate or freeze in covered containers. **Yield:** 4 pints.

RHUBARB CRISP
Blanche Comiskey, Franklin, Wisconsin

This versatile dessert is great served plain for breakfast, or as an after-dinner treat with ice cream. Either way, the flavor is terrific and seconds are tempting!

- 1 cup all-purpose flour
- 3/4 cup rolled oats
- 2 cups packed brown sugar, *divided*
- 1/4 teaspoon salt
- 1 teaspoon ground cinnamon
- 1/2 cup butter *or* margarine, melted
- 2 tablespoons cornstarch
- 1 cup water
- 1 teaspoon vanilla extract
- 4 cups sliced fresh *or* frozen rhubarb

In a bowl, combine flour, oats, 1 cup brown sugar, salt, cinnamon and butter. Pat about half of mixture onto the bottom of a greased 9-in. square baking pan. In a saucepan, combine cornstarch and remaining brown sugar; stir in water. Cook and stir until mixture comes to a boil and is thickened and clear. Remove from the heat; stir in vanilla. Add rhubarb and toss until coated. Spoon over crust; sprinkle with reserved flour mixture. Bake at 350° for 50 minutes or until bubbly. **Yield:** 9 servings.

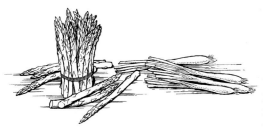

Creamy Cabbage, 63
German Coleslaw, 58
Goulash Soup, 6
Green Tomato Chowchow, 14
New England Boiled Dinner, 62
Nutty Coleslaw, 59
Overnight Slaw, 57
Peasant Soup, 58
Pickled Cabbage, 62
Stuffed Cabbage Rolls, 63
Red Cabbage with Apples, 57
Russian-Style Vegetable Soup, 62
Scalloped Cabbage, 59
Skillet Cabbage, 63
Spicy Cabbage Casserole, 58
Sweet-and-Sour Cabbage, 59
Tuna Crunch Casserole, 59
Vegetable Stew, 54

CAKES

Apple Walnut Cake, 76
Blueberry Sour Cream Pound
    Cake, 82
Butternut Squash Nut Cake, 22
Chocolate Zucchini Cake, 25
Coconut Apple Cake, 71
Fresh Apple Cake with Caramel
    Sauce, 77
Rhubarb Pudding Cake, 89
Zucchini Cake, 18

CAULIFLOWER

Broccoli and Cauliflower Salad, 50
Cauliflower and Wild Rice Soup, 51
Cauliflower Corn Supreme, 51
Cauliflower Ham Chowder, 49
Creamy Cauliflower Soup, 55
Marinated Vegetable Salad, 49
Vegetable Stew, 54

COLESLAW

Corn Slaw, 36
German Coleslaw, 58
Nutty Coleslaw, 59
Overnight Slaw, 57
Pickled Cabbage, 62

CONDIMENTS

Cranberry Salsa, 81
Cranberry Strawberry Sauce, 81
Herb Butter for Corn, 32
Mild Fresh Salsa, 6
Rhubarb Ketchup, 92
Rhubarb Steak Sauce, 93

Tomato-Garlic Dressing, 7
Tomato-Pepper Salsa, 12

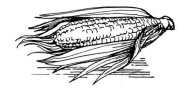

CORN

Boston Baked Corn, 28
Cauliflower Corn Supreme, 51
Cazuela, 27
Corn 'n' Cucumbers, 36
Corn and Spinach Souffle, 36
Corn Chowder, 27
Corn Cobbler, 29
Corn Hill Corn Bread, 34
Corn Medley, 37
Corn Relish, 29
Corn Slaw, 36
Corn-Stuffed Peppers, 34
Corn Vegetable Casserole, 37
Corn with Basil, 33
Corny Turkey Burgers, 32
Country Corncakes, 27
Crab and Corn Chowder, 46
Cream-Style Corn, 28
Double Corn Bake, 37
Down-Home Succotash, 32
Enchilada Casserole, 33
Fiesta Corn Salad, 32
Fresh Vegetable Kabobs, 33
Herb Butter for Corn, 32
"Hot" Corn Bread, 28
"Iowa in a Bowl", 34
Mexican Fried Corn, 36
Mexi-Corn Lasagna, 36
Patio Salad, 29
Red Corn Relish, 32
Roasted Corn and Avocado Dip, 29
Sage Corn Muffins, 28
Sausage Corn Chowder, 33
Succotash Salad, 33
Spicy Corn and Black Bean Relish, 37
Taco Soup, 34
Zesty Corn Custard, 28

CRANBERRIES

Cranberry-Orange Bars, 79
Cranberry Salsa, 81
Cranberry Strawberry Sauce, 81
Leftover Eggnog Cranberry
    Muffins, 80

DESSERTS
(also see Cakes and Pies)

Apple Gingerbread, 73
Berry Whirligig, 82
Blueberry-Peach Cobbler, 85

Cranberry-Orange Bars, 79
Cranberry Strawberry Sauce, 81
Creamy Rhubarb Dessert, 92
Grandma's Spring and Summer
    Torte, 88
Old-Fashioned Apple Crisp, 77
Oven-Fried Apples, 71
Peach and Blueberry Casserole, 85
Rhubarb Cobbler with Oat
    Dumplings, 89
Rhubarb Coconut Cookies, 90
Rhubarb Crisp, 93
Rhubarb Flip, 88
Rhubarb Peach Cobbler, 90
Rhubarb Pudding, 92
Russian Cream, 80
Schaum Torte, 85
Sliced Apple Fritters, 71
Stewed Rhubarb, 88
Strawberry Almondine, 84

GREEN BEANS

Hodgepodge Stew, 44
Red, White and Green Salad, 39
Summer Soup, 45

GREEN PEPPERS

Beef Tomato Stir-Fry, 15
Corn-Stuffed Peppers, 34
Garden Kabobs, 18
Gazpacho, 12
Green Tomato Chowchow, 14
Herbed Tomato and Cheese Salad, 14
Italian Garden Sauce, 11
Italian Zucchini Soup, 17
Pickled Tomato Salad, 11
Stuffed Green Peppers, 5
Tomato Beef and Rice Casserole, 15
Tomato Garden Casserole, 14
Tomato Pasta Salad, 7
Tomato-Pepper Salsa, 12
Tomato Pepper Steak, 10

JAMS & JELLIES

Raspberry Rhubarb Jam, 93
Rhubarb Marmalade, 90
Speedy Blueberry Refrigerator
    Jam, 85
Zucchini Peach Jelly, 19

MAIN DISHES

Acorn Cabbage Bake, 19
Asparagus and Ham Casserole, 67
Asparagus Salmon Pie, 67
Beef and Asparagus Skillet Dinner, 67
Beef Tomato Stir-Fry, 15
Broccoli Beef Curry, 50
Broccoli-Stuffed Potatoes, 51
Broccoli Tuna Roll-Ups, 50
Cazuela, 27
Chicken and Broccoli Roll-Ups, 55
Chicken/Asparagus Pasta Supper, 69
Corn-Stuffed Peppers, 34
Corny Turkey Burgers, 32
Double Corn Bake, 37
Enchilada Casserole, 33
Garden Kabobs, 18
Italian Garden Sauce, 11
Lamb Broccoli Strudel, 49
Mexican Taters and Beans, 41
Mexi-Corn Lasagna, 36
New England Boiled Dinner, 62
Red Rice, 6
Rhubarb Beef, 89
Spicy Cabbage Casserole, 58
Stuffed Cabbage Rolls, 63
Stuffed Green Peppers, 5
Tomato-Asparagus Souffle, 66
Tomato Beef and Rice Casserole, 15
Tomato Pepper Steak, 10
Tomato/Zucchini Pasta Supper, 15
Tuna Crunch Casserole, 59
Tuna-Stuffed Tomatoes, 14
Zucchini Hamburger Pie, 23
Zucchini Pizza, 22

MUFFINS & ROLLS

Apple Cinnamon Puffs, 72
Apple Nut Muffins, 73
Blueberry Muffins, 79
Broccoli Muffins, 54
Golden Squash Rolls, 25
Leftover Eggnog Cranberry
    Muffins, 80
Lemon-Raspberry Muffins, 80
Raspberry Muffins, 84
Rhubarb Muffins, 93
Sage Corn Muffins, 28

PEACHES

Blueberry-Peach Cobbler, 85
Peach and Blueberry Casserole, 85
Rhubarb Peach Cobbler, 90

PIES

Apple Praline Pie, 72
Blueberry Cream Pie, 81
Caramel Apple Pie, 72
Fresh Strawberry Pie, 79
Ozark Blue-Cranberry Pie, 84
Rhubarb Berry Pie, 88
Rhubarb Meringue Pie, 87
Three-Berry Pie with Crumb
    Topping, 80

POTATOES
(also see Sweet Potatoes)

Au Gratin Potatoes, 44
Bavarian Potato Soup, 47
Breakfast Potatoes, 40
Broccoli-Stuffed Potatoes, 51
Cabbage and Potato Side Dish, 58
California Potato Salad, 41
Cazuela, 27
Cheesy Potato Chowder, 41
Crab and Corn Chowder, 46
Delmonico Potatoes, 46
Garden Vegetable Soup, 46
German Potato Salad, 39
Goulash Soup, 6
Gourmet Potato Soup with
    Croutons, 46
Hodgepodge Stew, 44
Lamb and Potato Stew, 47
Mexican Taters and Beans, 41
New England Boiled Dinner, 62
New England Fish Chowder, 40
Potatas Forradas, 40
Potato Casserole, 39
Potato Frittata, 45
Potato Pancakes, 47
Potato Vegetable Quiche, 47
Ranch-Style Potato Salad, 44
Red, White and Green Salad, 39
Sheepherder's Potatoes, 40
Skier's Stew, 40
Spiced Potatoes, 44
Squash and Potatoes, 22
Summer Soup, 45
Vegetable Pancakes, 41
Vegetable Stew, 54

RASPBERRIES

Big Dutch Pancake with Little
    Berries, 85

Lemon-Raspberry Muffins, 80
Raspberry Cider, 82
Raspberry Muffins, 84
Raspberry Rhubarb Jam, 93
Rhubarb Berry Pie, 88
Three-Berry Pie with Crumb
    Topping, 80

RELISHES

Corn Relish, 29
Green Tomato Chowchow, 14
Green Tomato Mincemeat, 11
Red Corn Relish, 32
Rhubarb Relish, 93
Spicy Corn and Black Bean
    Relish, 37

RHUBARB

Baked Rhubarb, 89
Cherry Rhubarb Coffee Cake, 87
Creamy Rhubarb Dessert, 92
Grandma's Spring and Summer
    Torte, 88
Raspberry Rhubarb Jam, 93
Rhubarb Beef, 89
Rhubarb Berry Pie, 88
Rhubarb Cobbler with Oat
    Dumplings, 89
Rhubarb Coconut Cookies, 90
Rhubarb Crisp, 93
Rhubarb Flip, 88
Rhubarb Ketchup, 92
Rhubarb Peach Cobbler, 90
Rhubarb Pudding, 92
Rhubarb Pudding Cake, 89
Rhubarb Punch, 92
Rhubarb Marmalade, 90
Rhubarb Meringue Pie, 87
Rhubarb Muffins, 93
Rhubarb Relish, 93
Rhubarb Salad, 88
Rhubarb Steak Sauce, 93
Stewed Rhubarb, 88

SALADS *(Fruit)*

Apple-Strawberry Spinach Salad, 71
Rhubarb Salad, 88
Strawberry Apple Salad, 77
Taffy Apple Salad, 76

SALADS *(Vegetable)*

Asparagus Confetti Salad, 66
Asparagus Pasta Salad, 65
Asparagus-Tomato Salad, 65
Basil Broccoli/Tomato Platter, 54
Broccoli and Cauliflower Salad, 50
California Potato Salad, 41
Corn 'n' Cucumbers, 36
Festive Tomato Wedges, 5
Fiesta Corn Salad, 32
Garlic-Kissed Tomatoes, 14
German Potato Salad, 39
Herbed Tomato and Cheese Salad, 14
"Iowa in a Bowl", 34
Marinated Vegetable Salad, 49
Patio Salad, 29
Pickled Tomato Salad, 11
Picnic Zucchini Bean Salad, 18
Ranch-Style Potato Salad, 44
Red, White and Green Salad, 39
Succotash Salad, 33
Summer Spaghetti Salad, 5
Sweet-and-Sour Zucchini, 23
Sweet Potato Salad, 39
Tomato Pasta Salad, 7
Tortellini Vegetable Salad, 50
Zesty Tomato Zucchini Toss, 10

SIDE DISHES

Acorn Squash Rings, 23
Asparagus and Wild Rice
     Casserole, 66
Asparagus Tomato Bake, 67
Asparagus with Dill Butter, 69
Au Gratin Potatoes, 44
Autumn Casserole, 77
Baked Rhubarb, 89
Boston Baked Corn, 28
Broccoli-Onion Deluxe, 55
Broccoli-Stuffed Potatoes, 51
Butternut Squash Casserole, 22
Cabbage and Potato Side Dish, 58
Cabbage Au Gratin, 58
Cauliflower Corn Supreme, 51
Corn and Spinach Souffle, 36
Corn Cobbler, 29
Corn Medley, 37
Corn-Stuffed Peppers, 34
Corn Vegetable Casserole, 37
Corn with Basil, 33
Cream-Style Corn, 28
Creamy Cabbage, 63
Delmonico Potatoes, 46
Down-Home Succotash, 32

Dumplings with Tomatoes and
     Zucchini, 7
Fresh Vegetable Kabobs, 33
Fried Green Tomatoes, 7
Holiday Squash, 19
Holiday Sweet Potatoes, 45
Mexican Fried Corn, 36
Microwave Spaghetti Squash, 19
Potatas Forradas, 40
Potato Casserole, 39
Potato Pancakes, 47
Red Cabbage with Apples, 57
Scalloped Cabbage, 59
Skillet Cabbage, 63
Spiced Potatoes, 44
Squash and Potatoes, 22
Stuffed Garden Tomatoes, 10
Sweet-and-Sour Cabbage, 59
Sweet Potato Balls, 45
Tomato Garden Casserole, 14
Vegetable Pancakes, 41
Zucchini Patties, 23
Zucchini Provencal, 17

SOUPS & STEWS

Asparagus Cress Soup, 65
Bavarian Potato Soup, 47
Broccoli and Crab Bisque, 51
Broccoli Cheese Soup, 54
Cabbage Zucchini Borscht, 57
Cauliflower and Wild Rice Soup, 51
Cauliflower Ham Chowder, 49
Cheesy Potato Chowder, 41
Chunky Asparagus Soup, 66
Corn Chowder, 27
Crab and Corn Chowder, 46
Creamed Cabbage Soup, 63
Creamy Cauliflower Soup, 55
Creamy Tomato Bisque, 11
Curried Zucchini Soup, 18
Garden Vegetable Soup, 46
Gazpacho, 12
Goulash Soup, 6
Gourmet Potato Soup with
     Croutons, 46
Hodgepodge Stew, 44
Italian Zucchini Soup, 17
Lamb and Potato Stew, 47
Lentil Soup, 6
New England Fish Chowder, 40
Peasant Soup, 58
Quick Zesty Chili, 12
Russian-Style Vegetable Soup, 62

Sausage Corn Chowder, 33
Skier's Stew, 40
Summer Soup, 45
Taco Soup, 34
Tomato Leek Soup, 15
Tomato Mushroom Soup, 7
Tomato Vegetable Soup, 6
Vegetable Stew, 54
Zucchini Bisque, 18

SQUASH

Acorn Cabbage Bake, 19
Acorn Squash Rings, 23
Butternut Squash Nut Cake, 22
Butternut Squash Casserole, 22
Cabbage Zucchini Borscht, 57
Cazuela, 27
Chocolate Zucchini Cake, 25
Corn Medley, 37
Curried Zucchini Soup, 18
Dumplings with Tomatoes and
     Zucchini, 7
Fresh Vegetable Kabobs, 33
Garden Kabobs, 18
Golden Squash Rolls, 25
Holiday Squash, 19
Italian Zucchini Soup, 17
Microwave Spaghetti Squash, 19
Onion Zucchini Bread, 17
Picnic Zucchini Bean Salad, 18
Pumpkin Zucchini Bread, 25
Squash and Potatoes, 22
Sweet-and-Sour Zucchini, 23
Tomato/Zucchini Pasta Supper, 15
Zesty Tomato Zucchini Toss, 10
Zucchini Bisque, 18
Zucchini Cake, 18
Zucchini Hamburger Pie, 23
Zucchini Patties, 23
Zucchini Peach Jelly, 19
Zucchini Pizza, 22
Zucchini Provencal, 17
Zucchini Spread, 25

STRAWBERRIES

Apple-Strawberry Spinach Salad, 71
Big Dutch Pancake with Little
     Berries, 85
Cranberry Strawberry Sauce, 81
Fresh Strawberry Pie, 79
Rhubarb Berry Pie, 88
Schaum Torte, 85
Strawberry Almondine, 84

SWEET POTATOES

TOMATOES

  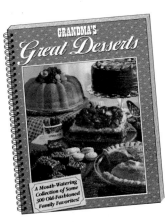